CRISIS IN
MUSLIM EDUCATION

General Editor   Syed Ali Ashraf

CRISIS IN
MUSLIM EDUCATION

Syed Sajjad Husain
and
Syed Ali Ashraf

HODDER AND STOUGHTON

KING ABDULAZIZ UNIVERSITY, JEDDAH

Husain, Syed Sajjad
    Crisis in Muslim education. – (Islamic education
    series).
    1. Islam – Education
    I. Title   II. Ashraf, Syed Ali   III. Series
    370'.917'671   LC903

    ISBN 0-340-23608-6

First published 1979
Copyright © 1979 King Abdulaziz University, Jeddah

Phototypeset in V.I.P. Baskerville by Western Printing Services
Ltd, Bristol. Printed in Great Britain for Hodder and Stoughton
Educational, a division of Hodder and Stoughton Ltd., Mill
Road, Dunton Green, Sevenoaks, Kent by Hazell Watson &
Viney Ltd, Aylesbury, Bucks.

Contents

Foreword

بسم الله الرحمن الرحيم

The Muslim World is passing through a transition period of tremendously fast geo-political transformation and of rapid social change. God-given wealth has brought both worldly prestige and unforeseen worries. In order to cope with these problems and at the same time save the Muslim world from being over-run or controlled by alien ideas and forces, the authorities had to learn and teach modern knowledge in all its forms. Along with this came modern Western methodology and Western secular concepts dominating all branches of knowledge. The rapidity with which expansion of education was considered necessary made it extremely difficult for authorities to wait till Islamic concepts were evolved by Muslim scholars.

But by the grace of Allah Muslim scholars have become aware of the consequence of these concepts and the way brainwashing is effected by Western methodology. King Abdulaziz University therefore organized the First World Conference on Muslim Education. It was held in the holy city of Mecca from 31 March to 8 April, 1977 12–20 Rabiuttani, 1937 A.H., in order to discuss this problem and find ways and means of evolving Islamic concepts and of creating Islamic methodology.

I am glad that Dr. Ashraf, the organizing secretary of that Conference, has now succeeded in having edited and published all the valuable papers submitted at the Conference.

In the present volume he and Dr Husain have presented in a nutshell the problems faced by us. This book provides a valuable introduction to the rest of the books in this series. Allah willing, King Abdulaziz University will take all necessary steps in the future to see that solutions are intellectually formulated and practically applied.

Jeddah
22 Shawwal, 1398 A.H.

Abdullah Omar Naseef
Vice-Rector
King Abdulaziz University,
Jeddah

Acknowledgements

We acknowledge with thanks permission granted by the following authorities to edit and print portions of chapters already printed in journals or books: *The Times* for 'The Introduction' and an extract from Prof. Naquib-al-Attas's article. They were printed in *The Times Education Supplement* (4 April, 1977) and *The Times* (31 March, 1977) respectively; *Impact* for portions of Chapter I printed under the title 'Tradition and Modernity in the Muslim world'; Harvard University Press and Professor Hosein Nasr for permission to reprint extracts from *Science and Civilization in Islam* by Dr. Nasr published by Harvard University Press.

Preface

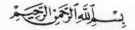

Education is a process involving three references: the individual, the society or national community to which he or she belongs, and the whole content of reality, both material and spiritual, which plays a dominant role in determining the nature and destiny of Man and Society. All important Eastern and Western educationists agree that the 'aim of education is a question that admits of no answer without a reference to ultimate convictions about human nature and destiny, about society and how the individual stands in relation to it'. Education, they all agree, is a continuous process necessary for the full and balanced development of persons. But the interpretations of the secularists, Marxists and religious thinkers vary. It is this variation which is creating conflicts in the modern world. When the Muslim world started modernising itself, it began to be invaded by non-Marxist 'liberal' and 'Marxists' concepts. From the doctrinal point of view it has been easier to resist Marxist ideas but it has become rather difficult to counteract the influences of Western 'liberalism' because all branches of knowledge have been affected by it and also because Muslim scholars have not as yet formulated Islamic concepts as substitutes for liberal concepts. The greatest danger of liberal education is the creation of a bewildering variety of ideas and thoughts. As a critic of 'liberal education' has recently said, 'There is no certain way to guarantee the survival of past values.' Dr. Rothblatt in his historical analysis of liberal education, *Tradition and Change in English Liberal Education*, concludes that the 'continual metamorphosis' of the relationship between liberal education and knowledge and the production of various 'philosophical schema' have practically destroyed the historical relationship between 'society, education and self'. What has happened in the West is definitely going to happen to the Muslim world if we Muslim scholars cannot resist this 'moth-eaten liberalism'. Islam has given the world a philosophy which gives standards of value and judgement that apply to all spheres and activities of human life. Unless that philosophy succeeds in broadening its range of application and in giving Islamic concepts for all branches of knowledge, it will not be able to satisfy new generations and save them from the invasion of divided purposes and paralysing doubts. The permissiveness of the West will help the Marxists to conquer the minds of younger generations because in Marxism there is a dogma, a conceptual stability and a utopian goal.

Muslim scholars met in the holy city of Mecca in 1977 to discuss this crisis. This book is an attempt to help readers to explore different aspects of that crisis. The remarkable similarity of ideas and a common approach that became evident have encouraged the writers of this book to highlight the problems and draw the attention of all those scholars, thinkers and organizers of education who think alike and are at present engaged in research. Extracts from the papers presented at the First World Conference on Muslim Education have been added to each chapter in order to indicate the common approach and the variety of problems envisaged by the participants. All the issues treated in detail in the other books in this series have been presented in this book in a general way so that the challenges that have been thrown to accepted assumptions in the other books in this series may be presented in the context of the changing society.

This book is a joint product. Dr. Ashraf was responsible for writing the Introduction, and chapters I, IV, V and the 'Notes' and Dr. Husain for writing chapters II, III, VI and VII. Though they have written different chapters they are both committed to all the views expressed in the book. They jointly selected and edited the extracts.

Syed Ali Ashraf
General Editor

Introduction

Islamic Education is an education which trains the sensibility of pupils in such a manner that in their attitude to life, their actions, decisions and approach to all kinds of knowledge, they are governed by the spiritual and deeply felt ethical values of Islam. They are trained, and mentally so disciplined, that they want to acquire knowledge not merely to satisfy an intellectual curiosity or just for material worldly benefit, but to develop as rational, righteous beings and bring about the spiritual, moral and physical welfare of their families, their people and mankind. This attitude derives from a deep faith in God and a whole-hearted acceptance of a God-given moral code. The permanence, necessity and significance of such a code for the natural development of a rational and spiritual man is experienced and understood by the application of those principles in Nature and society. A student who receives an Islamic education grows up peace-loving, harmonious, equable and righteous with faith and trust in God's infinite mercy and His invincible justice, and lives in harmony and not conflict, with Nature. He also believes that man is not only a creature of this earth but a spiritual being, gifted with limitless and inestimable power to control and govern the universe under the authority of God; a being whose life extends beyond this world into a region where his own consciousness fully reasserts itself and makes him realize the effect of his actions on his own being. Thus he gains pleasure from doing good and he dislikes or even hates, acts of evil because he realizes the effects of his actions on his own conscience.

It is obvious that this type of education cannot be imparted easily in any society which has lost its religious moorings. This is what has happened so frequently in the West. Though there are various religious groups in Europe and America carrying on missionary activities, neither the authorities in their societies nor most of their intellectuals accept a religious code as an inevitable and unquestioned norm providing them with ethical and spiritual assumptions. Since the Renaissance this process of moral decline has continued and in the twentieth century

1

intellectuals have succeeded in breaking loose from what they considered their bondage. Education has been the most effective method of changing the attitudes of the young and thus leading them to accept and initiate social change. Modern Western education places an exaggerated emphasis upon reason and rationality and underestimates the value of the spirit. It encourages scientific enquiry at the expense of faith; it promotes individualism; it breeds scepticism; it refuses to accept that which is not demonstrable; it is anthropocentric rather than theocentric. Even where it does not directly challenge faith, it relegates it to the background as something much less important than reason. The result is that the intellectuals have become at variance with one another, each individual claiming his philosophy to be the only correct guidance for himself and sometimes propounding it with missionary zeal for others. When such an individual philosophy catches the mind of a powerful group it is turned into a dogma. Marxism is one such philosophy. For the sake of security in a rootless society some people have accepted this new dogma and with religious fervour they have turned their society into a dogma-controlled community.

It can be seen that religious groups are no longer dominating the social scene in the West and hence all branches of knowledge have no central, integrating force. That is why after the Second World War the Presidents of American Universities met in Harvard University in 1957 and divided knowledge into three branches – Humanities, Natural Sciences and Social Sciences. They left out Divinity and decided on a core curriculum for all undergraduates who were required to take at least one course from each of the three. They thought that in this way they would be able to build in each student an all-round Democratic personality. This means they believed that Democracy provided a complete solution for society. But what of Man's spiritual cravings? What about the relationship that exists between spiritual realization and the essence of moral values? What about the integral relationship between moral values and human action in a social and cultural set-up? Can Democracy take the place of religion?

These questions have not been answered nor can they be answered when society is suffering from rootlessness. The Muslim World too has been invaded by this Western form of civilization. This feeling of rootlessness has already entered Muslim society because our intellectuals are now being educated in the West, being brainwashed and returning to their own countries after reading text-books which are all filled with ideas in conflict with their traditional assumptions. Even in Muslim countries the traditional Islamic education system has been

2

superseded by a modern one which has been borrowed from the West. As a result text-books and courses and even methods of teaching are creating doubts in the minds of the students about the fundamental tenets and assumptions of Islam instead of reinforcing faith in God and purifying the sensibility by removing confusion and contradiction.

At first the traditionally learned class, the 'ulama, resisted this system and tried to save Muslim society by preserving the traditional system of education. But as they did not at the same time try to meet the challenge to religion coming from secular concepts they could only preserve the spiritual concept in a section of the community. Hence, 'a cultural duality appeared everywhere in the Muslim world, a duality in society that resulted from the dual education systems; the traditional Islamic education system creating the traditional Islamic group, and the modern secular education system creating the secularists. In many regions a secular education system gradually replaced all other forms of education. In other regions both systems are still in existence but the secular system has become the more dominant.'

Unfortunately, neither the traditionalists nor the modernists, neither the political authorities nor the traditionally learned class, ever tried to evolve a common system through which the transmission of values could be integrated with the development of new skills and techniques, and faith could be strengthened through the production and distribution of wealth. As a result the two motivations – the maintenance and strengthening of spiritual values, and the material prosperity and industrial advancement of society – have pulled the different sections of society apart. The traditional system of education is resisting change but preserving spiritual values, and modern education is ignoring the inroads into values through Western text-books and methodology.

There is a realization even among those who have gone through the process of modern education, both educators and students, that this 'crisis' of group conflicts based on ideological differences ought to be removed if the cultural identity of the Muslims is to be preserved and strengthened. Gradual political regeneration of the Muslim world has further intensified this effort.

It is further realized that if the intellectuals of the Muslim world do not stem the tide now by instilling Islamic concepts in all branches of knowledge and changing the methodology from unbridled questioning to the exploration of the significance of everything for the sake of understanding Human life and External Nature, the time is not far away when the tide will sweep away even the bed-rock on which the structure of Muslim society is based. The method which traditional Muslim society and, in fact, any religious-based society should adopt in order to preserve itself, is acceptance of values and experiential reality based on that acceptance and the application in active life of the realization of Truth through experience. The method that modern education and modern civilization use is questioning without any accepted norm, and the collection of data on the basis of which answers are found or discovered. Thus, according to our traditional method, society's foundation is seen to be morally sound whereas according to modern thought, it is disturbed by individual realizations which are almost always conflicting, heterogeneous and goalless. Muslim intellectuals are expected now to justify their methods and at the same time restate their traditional ideas in the context of the new, and formulate new concepts for recent branches of knowledge by reasserting the spiritual realization of Truth as enshrined in revelations from God. That these revelations have within them the source of all kinds of knowledge for the benefit of mankind has to be shown to modern man in order to convince him of the unending potentialities of Islam.

This challenge is now one for modern intellectuals. It is this new intellectual class which guides and governs the minds of younger generations. Therefore educational reform is necessary. This is not just the reform of basic concepts of sociology, economics, political science, psychology, and history but a rewriting of text-books on the basis of Islamic concepts. It is a gigantic task.

That was why King Abdulaziz University, Jeddah and Mecca, Saudi Arabia, organized the first World Conference on Muslim Education which was held in Mecca from 31 March to 8 April, 1977. Out of the papers presented in Mecca, we have culled those extracts where the above crisis has been clearly indicated and some solutions suggested. This book is an introduction to the study of those methods by which the crisis could be resolved, both the content and the methodology of Islamic education revised and vitalized, and a new direction provided as to the method of integrating the traditional and modern systems of education.

For the whole Western secular world, this experiment will be extremely valuable if the Muslim world can show the efficacy of these concepts in the form of intellectual growth without any loss of emotional stability that faith in a God-given code provides. This may thus open the eyes of secularists and strike a responsive chord in their hearts. They may begin to think afresh of Man and his nature and also rethink the necessity of providing sustenance to the human spirit. A large number of those Western men and women who are trying to get such sustenance from various forms of spiritual practice may come to believe in the importance and significance of a complete code of life such as Islam provides.

Chapter One

Education and Culture in the Muslim World: Conflict between Tradition and Modernity

The Muslim World

The term 'Muslim World' refers to the area whose inhabitants are predominantly Muslim. This area extends from Morocco to Indonesia with two gaps one filled by people who are predominantly Hindu – in India and Thailand – and the other co-extensive with China and Japan and Tibet, which still owes cultural allegiance to some form of Buddhism. The rest of the world is predominantly Christian though other forces such as Communism and modern scientific humanism have already made severe inroads into it. The traditional centres of the Muslim world are still Mecca and Medina. People may not practise Islam with that kind of fervour that prevailed among Muslims in the early days of Islam, but the basic categories of judgement and the unquestioned assumptions of what is meant by goodness and who is a good Muslim, are still drawn from Islam. It is true that in certain areas the ruling authorities have constitutionally replaced their norm of Islam by 'secularism' and in many places in North Africa, authorities have been rather silent about religion. But the way of life is still intrinsically Islamic. It is the intelligentsia and the ruling powers who have tried to secularize these countries for reasons which will be discussed later.

Culture and Civilization

Culture is an extremely difficult word to define. It is necessary for us to differentiate it from civilization. Civilization is an evolving process. It is a product of human curiosity which compels man to acquire more and more knowledge for its own sake and also utilize that knowledge in actual life. This utilization leads to the production of technology which, Toynbee rightly points out, is 'coeval with Man'.[1] Whatever he learns he applies. Hence there is a constant process of improvement in the

7

instruments of civilization. Language is the means by which man goes on preserving and transmitting this knowledge and thus all his traditions of the past are being continuously modified. Language is constantly changing: it can never remain static without dying. That is why, even when two succeeding generations concur in preserving the same tradition, it can never be transmitted from one generation to the next without some involuntary change taking place. Moreover, as man is a technological animal – constantly applying the knowledge acquired by him in order to change, modify and transform his environment and the social pattern of his generation – the form and organization of his society are in a constant process of change. Nurture plays a very important role in social life. History, which Toynbee defines as 'the study of how and why one situation changes into another'[2] is replete with examples of social change, technological improvement and deliberate or involuntary transformation. From time immemorial the instruments of civilization have been improved and hence its social organization has become more and more complex.

The Role of Religion

In spite of constant change in social traditions, unbroken series of improvements in technology and desirable, or undesirable, complexities in the nature of civilization, there is an immutable factor in Man: his spirit. This spirit is always in search of permanence and the absolute. It is never satisfied with the changing environment. It always penetrates behind and beyond the changing façade of social patterns and seeks the eternal, the essential, the immutable. In different periods and ages various aspects of human personality have been emphasized; consequently the concepts of personality propagated by different eminent and influential philosophers have differed but the basic nature of man never changes. That man's spirit is in search of the eternal, that he always sees the timeless within time, is demonstrated by the incommensurability and absoluteness of great works of art and by the fact that people of different ages can appreciate the drawings of cave-men or the epics of Homer, Firdausi and Valmiki. Had man's nature been changed by nurture, had social organization been able to transform the basic nature of man, it would have been impossible for a modern man to appreciate Shakespeare or the Noh plays of Japan. We can easily respond to these works of art only because of their emphasis on that constant factor: the spirit of Man. That is why we cannot say that Bertrand Russell was more cultured than Socrates though in comparison with the civilization of today, the civilization of Athens of those days must be regarded as primitive. Culture, therefore, is based on the findings of this spirit of man. These findings are the result of three essential, stable and immutable ingredients of that spirit: man's power to choose between this and that, which implies man's spiritual ability to distinguish between this and that, and thus his consciousness of himself, others and the universe; man's recognition of a norm of values which is so intimately ingrained in his nature that even a child can differentiate between truth and falsehood, and react favourably to justice and sharply against injustice. The third factor is the demand for the absolute in all forms. It is this search for the absolute that leads man to discover under the paraphernalia of the instruments of civilization the essence of himself and portray them in caves or on paper, or in literature and art. It is this search for the absolute that is manifested through religion. Religion is the product of the contact between the absolute in Man with the absolute that is immanent in the universe and Man and that transcends them at the same time. Civilization affects culture only by its partial emphasis on certain elements which the condition of a particular society at a particular moment compels man to emphasize. Therefore there is a progression in civilization but there is only a rise and fall in the culture of man both in the world as a whole and in so far as certain groups of people are concerned. Those who lose touch with the increasing expansion and complexity of the instruments of civilization become backward or remain underdeveloped. But even these underdeveloped nations or societies may be culturally highly advanced. But taking mankind as a whole and looking at the history of human civilization we may safely conclude that because of man's increasing command over technology, human civilization is showing continuous progress. But as technology is not the essence of humanity and as culture is integrally related to the immutable and absolute norm of values, advancement in civilization does not necessarily indicate advancement in culture. Toynbee, after his survey of human history, has concluded that those features on which man's existence, survival and well-being depend 'cannot appear directly in archaeological records, since they are not material but are spiritual'.[3] Even an irreligious philosopher like Bertrand Russell comes to practically the same conclusion in the last chapter of his book, *Impact of Science on Society*. Science and technology, he finds, are neutral disciplines leading mankind to such a complex intellectual field that he feels it necessary to evoke the Christian concept of charity and love in order to preserve humanity.[4]

Muslim Culture

Muslim culture must be seen in the light of this dichotomy of culture and civilization and in the context of modern civilization. The essence of Muslim culture is drawn from the most comprehensive and the most liberal norm of values that mankind has so far seen – the norm that accepts all the previous norms and provides an all-absorbing scheme for human life and ideals. It adds to all previous disciplines in this field by stressing another source of Truth and Knowledge, man's spiritual ability to realize wisdom (*hikmat*) from the Absolute. This knowledge is not acquired by intellect but is given to man. When we accept the existence of our will to choose, we must also accept the presence of that Will in the entire universe. God's Will is operative in this universe. 'Revelation' was the result of the contact of the individual will with the Supreme Universal Will. God revealed His Will for the benefit of man through the Will of that individual whom God had chosen as His Prophet. The absolute that man seeks is realized through this contact. The absolute norm is therefore derived from this contact through what is regarded in Islam as the attributes of God. All varied kinds of existence manifest different qualities and all qualities are derived from the same Absolute reality. Man is regarded by Islam as the Vicegerent of Allah on Earth and the entire 'creation' is regarded as subservient to man.[5] His is the vicegerent or representative of God on the Earth because God has bestowed on him, and him alone among all created things, the most comprehensive ability to recognize, understand and emulate the attributes of God and realize them in practice in this life. Only because of this comprehensiveness is there no limit to human knowledge and no end to human ability to command the universe. But because man is not the creator of these qualities and because the only universal and all-comprehensive Will is the Will of God, for the complete fructification of human personality, the norm of the attributes must be obeyed. Only then can human nature find fulfilment.

That is why Islam does not say that all other religions are untrue. On the other hand Islam asserts that as God is One and all mankind His 'supreme' creation, there is only one religion[6] and there is not a single human habitation where God did not send his messenger, to use a

Quranic expression. It is also said that only later followers of that religion interpolated new and foreign ideas, ideas not derived from any contact with the Absolute, but from man's limited knowledge, and thus created false or misleading dimensions of the Original religion. Historically to some extent this may be verified by saying that monotheistic Hinduism as seen in the Upanishadas was transformed in a much later period into the polytheism of the Puranas – the polytheism that is practised among the masses in India and Java, a polytheism which Hindu sanyasies always discard. A Muslim is therefore asked to believe in the purity of all the prophets and never speak ill of any religion.[7]

It is out of this basic norm provided by the Quran and the Sunnah, or the action and sayings of the Prophet of Islam, that a way of life emerged. It is that way of life which gave birth to a large number of institutions of different sorts. Through traditional education and through these socio-cultural institutions such as maktabs, madrasahs, mosques, jurisprudence and zawiyas the Muslims of the past tried to preserve their way of life. Education was the best means of preserving and transmitting that way of life because through education an implicit acceptance of the norm of values was achieved. The basic norm was never questioned by Muslim thinkers and scientists. This unquestioned acceptance did not prevent them from exploring vast fields of knowledge. Because God is the source of knowledge, by knowing more they felt that they were drawing nearer to God. As they did not start from a negative premise, they did not have to generalize on the basis of their limited range of findings, they also did not presume to build up new hypotheses.

Primordial Tradition versus Changing Attitudes

Traditional society still forms the basic core of the Muslim world. It still believes in the *Revelations* stored in the Quran and looks to the Sunnah for interpretation and guidance. It finds in these the primordial traditions and the norm of values with the help of which it sets up the ideal of the 'good man' and the 'good life'. It examines the history of Muslim civilization in its early days in order to provide its members with ideals and patterns of life. These patterns infuse all facets of life with significance and purpose. The value structure generates collective energy towards a purposeful goal. Society thus achieves coherence within diversity, a commonly accepted symbolism in the form of

11

religious and social events such as the Aquiqah and the Bismillah ceremony, Friday congregational prayer, Ashura, Hajj, Fasting in the month of Ramadan, the Eid Festivals and Qurbani. Muslim imagination is thus dominated by some primordial images or archetypes such as the Prophet himself, the Hero, the Saint or Sufi, and the Repentant. The traditional society therefore, loves those institutions which help it to preserve and maintain that structure and turn it into a logical hierarchy of values. Thus the co-ordination of social action in a traditional society is possible because of the value attached to these institutions (such as the mosque, the sufis, the 'ulama and the madrasah) and a common concept of life. The international character of these institutions and these images, and the primordial character of the tradition, give to this Muslim world a common purpose and common mechanism of communication.

It is in the twentieth century that the basic norm has been challenged or by-passed. This is a universal phenomenon because it is a product of modern technology which has almost got out of man's hands and has started controlling man's body and soul like a Frankenstein. Industrialization has led to urbanization, complexity of production and distribution, and the increasing necessity of centralization. Better medical facilities have led to overpopulation and this in its turn to various processes of controlling birth and causing death. The dissociation of the spiritual aspect of birth and death has given rise to a purely mundane attitude to sexual relationship and the control of birth. Centralization has compelled man to depend more and more on experts; thus individual understanding has been correspondingly minimized. New means of propaganda are making governments more and more aware of the ability to control the mind of man. Hence the widespread use of radio and television. Brainwashing is going on continuously. The secularist forces released by secular education and secular thinking generated by a modern scientific approach have made man empirical in attitude and doubtful about the need to think in terms of religion. All these have started neutralizing the hierarchy of values and Sharia is ignored and not enforced. Religious instruction in schools does not provide a deterrent because all other text-books are pervaded by secularist ideas generated in the West. New economists, the political elite and the literary elite weaken the religious, traditional bonds and concepts. It is not surprising therefore that the undermining of religious convictions and the neutralization of the heirarchy of values should lead to an upsurge of the common socio-cultural and secularist tendencies that draw their sustenance from narrow regional concepts.

Thus a chasm has been created between 'traditional' and 'modern' society.

This chasm is widening because we have accepted urbanization and industrialization as our goals without even waiting to consider those cultural implications involved in such a decision. Competition with Western countries and the lure of material progress have led the dominant section of these countries to court this change. Urbanization and industrialization are proceeding at a rapid pace, too rapid for traditional society to adjust itself to the changes that are flooding Muslim countries.

The Muslim world did not have time to think over the complexities that it was courting. The entire emphasis of all those countries which openly chose secularism was on material advancement. Other Muslim countries have followed their lead without openly advocating secularism but accepting it in the garb of a superficial and even bastard compromise. They have all tried to achieve economic modernization through industrialization and have thus committed themselves almost unconditionally to the transformation of the traditional paternalistic agrarian society into a modern, intellectual, secular, technological society. But the pull of tradition has forced some of these countries to declare their countries as Islamic states and/or introduce religious instruction as an item on the secular educational set-up at whose apex is an entirely areligious modern university. Knowledge and virtue used to go hand in hand in the traditional education system. Not only did the students acquire worldly knowledge, they were also trained intellectually and emotionally to be religious. There was no objection to scientific knowledge but the scientists believed that by acquiring knowledge about the phenomenal world they were only strengthening their belief in the greatness and power of the Creator. In other words they were not undermining religious assumptions and never felt the need to formulate new hypotheses. In the present system knowledge is an intellectual acquisition which may or may not have direct relationship with the traditional concepts of virtue. We have thus imported from Western sociology scientific assumptions and hypotheses and sociological analyses of life and conflicting formulations which are directly contradictory to our traditional religious assumptions. As a result 'hypocrisy' has become a public style and anxiety is increasing.

There is also growing polarization in the economic condition of various classes. In some countries monopolistic capitalism has grown so rapidly that it has not been adjusted to the traditional concepts of social investment and virtuous action in the forms of Zakat, Sadaqa and

13

other forms of charity. Various avenues of technical training and education, and the heavy emphasis on individual competition and laissez-faire, have laid a premium on manipulative and worldly-ambitious citizens. The result is the demand for a complete change and the growth of socialism in some form or other. As yet in no Muslim country has there been an attempt to put into practice an economic system in which the basic religious concepts of social justice, the religious principles of equal opportunity for all, of equity and of an interestless economy incorporate within its framework the religious injunctions of *Zakat*. This would have eliminated the dangers of two forms of capitalism – individual capitalism which secures freedom of the individual but indirectly compels the individual to be subservient to others and state capitalism which can never succeed without severely curtailing individual freedom, in some cases without eliminating this freedom.

As a result in all the Muslim countries the old 'established' society in which virtue, family traditions and religious authority and in some cases tribal glory used to have a premium put on them is being replaced by a new urban society in which the individual is regarded less as a human being within a family or tribe and more as a legal abstraction having rights, privileges and duties. This has given rise to insecurity and tension, often degenerating into conflict. This tension led to a bloodbath in Indonesia and other Muslim countries.

Industrialization has brought in polarization of income and this has led to the emergence of socialist parties and in many states to state capitalism. Modern education has encouraged the scientific attitude to life and hence secularism and individualism. It has also created a large wage-earning proletariat and advanced worldliness even to the point of hedonism. Because of the need for central control it has led to the emergence of a power-conscious central authority, be that authority bureaucrats under a Dictator or under a Party Boss. It has also created an industrial elite, as well as a political elite in a hurry, enterprising, cost-conscious, scientific-minded but mostly lacking in spirituality. Individually a large number of people are religious in their personal behaviour but as yet any attempt to synthesize modernity with the traditional approach to life has been rather timid. There are signs that everywhere in the West a large section of Muslim scholars and students has become conscious of the present state of affairs and they are trying to organize themselves. So far this organization has remained more of an academic than of a practical nature.

Traditional culture and attitudes to life are thus in conflict with modernity. This conflict is tearing apart not only the old and the young but also the traditionalists and modernists among the young. This group-conflict is affecting the character of society. Those who are devoted to religion are in conflict with those who are more or less secular in attitude. Regionalism is in conflict with nationalism, and nationalism with the traditional Muslim feeling that unites a Muslim in any part of the world with the supra-national Islamic Ummah. Institutions have sprung up which are alien to traditional Islamic instructions and concepts. Dance institutes, dramatic clubs, the cinema and the mode of fashions that cinemas and theatres encourage, state-sponsored cocktail parties, ladies' fashions that contradict and openly violate the Quranic principles of dress – all these indicate the emergence of a new character which is either non-religious, irreligious or anti-religious in most of its manners and attitudes. In each case these new institutions or complexes indicate subservience to the secularized section of the West from whom we have borrowed the scientific world view and modern attitude to life. Hence more and more stress is laid on the division of human activities into worldly and religious. Religion is now said to belong to the spirit only. Islam on the other hand teaches mankind that each and every human activity must be regarded as a form of worship. It says that it is the spirit of man that unifies his physical, mental, emotional and spiritual self, restores balance and maintains its relevant proportions and strength. Too much emphasis on intellect and body – and the denial, rejection or the ignoring of the spiritual character of Man – have naturally led to imbalance and conflict within the mind of most young Muslims today and within the body politic among extremists.

It is difficult to resolve this conflict if the traditional religious attitude is either discarded or ignored in favour of the empirical, because this will magnify conflicts and lead possibly to further bloodshed. Those disciplined in the old systems and not fully aware of the complexities of modern civilization, and those disciplined in the new system who have never cared to appreciate their own heritage, can never come together or resolve the conflict. All attempts in the past have proved false and hypocritical. The traditionalists either exploited the name of religion for irreligious purposes or were exploited by the modernists for their own secular ends. What is therefore necessary is the emergence of a third group who are acquainted with their own traditions but are willing to acquire any wisdom that modern civilization can offer. Only then will it be possible for a modern Muslim to integrate the principles of moral and spiritual behaviour with current intellectual knowledge.

Neither the first nor the second group can preserve today the organic and creative character of our society. By ignoring either modern life or the experiences of modern man, or by discarding the religious ideals which supply society with a moral framework and a goal, both groups make 'the co-ordination of social action impossible' to use an expression of Karl Mannheim. This is what he calls 'a kaleidoscopic concept of life'.[8] It is only this third group that can preserve the organic character of our society and save it from the malaise of modern Western civilization; that of dehumanization and of cohesion through the loss of those common situations and images which form a society and bind its members together.

People belonging to this third group, however, are still to a large extent disjointed and extremely limited in number. As they have to work within the context of modern life, they have to 'reconstruct' protective philosophical and theological systems and reinterpret religious thought in terms of modern life. Only when this is completed will they be able to save modern Muslims from the Nothingness that modern man in the West is facing. Along with this they will have to work out a comprehensive political, social and economic framework suitable for modern man but essentially Islamic in character. Only by doing this will they be able to save modern Muslims from the tension and insecurity in which they are living today.

Educational Remedy

Education is the best means of creating a new generation of young men and women who will not lose touch with their own tradition but who will not at the same time become intellectually retarded or educationally backward or unaware of developments in any branch of human knowledge.[9] Unfortunately such a system of education is not yet prevalent in any of the Muslim countries.

There are at present two systems of education. The first, traditional, which has confined itself to classical knowledge, has not shown any keen interest in new branches of knowledge that have emerged in the West nor in new methods of acquiring knowledge important in the Western system of education. This system is valuable therefore for classical theological knowledge but even the classical theologians produced by this system are not equipped with either intellectual knowledge or a method of meeting the challenges of a modern Godless technological civilization. The second system of education imported into Muslim countries, fully subscribed to and supported by all governmental authorities, is one borrowed from the West. At the head of this system is the modern University which is totally secular and hence non-religious in its approach to knowledge. Unfortunately, these people educated by this new system of education, known as modern education, are generally unaware of their own tradition and classical heritage. It is also not possible for this group to provide such leadership as we have envisaged in the earlier section.

The creation of a third system embracing an integrated system of education, is necessary but integration is not an easy process. Nor is it justifiable when integration might lead to a total elimination of the traditional system of education, or the lowering of the status of that system to such an extent that people would look down on it, or ignore those who would specialize in that branch. This matter has been dealt with in a later chapter but here all that we want to emphasize is the fact that the Western system of modern education is a secularized form which needs immediate reform. Such reform would aim to save society both from political tension between the two different factions, the traditionalists and the modernists, and also from secularization and the creation of tension and lack of purpose in society which the West is suffering from.

There have been various discussions and writings in the past and even attempts to remove this dichotomy and Islamicize modern education, but they have not succeeded because the rest of the problem has never been tackled. The intensification of the crisis that we face today in our society and in our education system stems from this failure. Though there have been attempts to make religious education compulsory there has been no attempt so far to teach literature and fine arts, social sciences and natural sciences from the Islamic point of view. As a result what children have been learning from religion has been contradicted by what is given to them through the humanities or social sciences and natural sciences. Unless an attempt is made now to Islamicize the humanities, social, and natural sciences by producing basic concepts and by changing the methodology of approaching them or teaching them, it will not be possible to create a viable group intellectually capable of resisting the onslaught of secularist teaching.

Extracts

1. The Cultural Predicament

(i) Dualism in the West and its resultant scepticism
Dr. Syed Muhammad al-Naquib al-Attas: from *Preliminary Thoughts on the Nature of Knowledge and the Definition and Aims of Education*, pp. 1–4

Dr. Syed Muhammad al-Naquib Al-Attas, philosopher, linguist and educationist, is Professor and Director of the Institute of Malay Language, Literature and Culture in the National University of Malaysia, Kuala Lumpur. His analysis of the nature of knowledge and the aims of Islamic education is emphatic in its assertion of a definite Islamic guiding philosophy. He is of the view that the concept of knowledge underlying Western civilization poses a threat to civilization itself.

What is the character and personality, the essence and spirit of Western civilization that has so transformed both itself and the world, bringing all who accept its interpretation of knowledge to a state of chaos leading to the brink of disaster? By 'Western civilization' I mean the civilization that has evolved out of the historical fusion of cultures, philosophies, values and aspirations of ancient Greece and Rome; their amalgamation with Judaism and Christianity, and their further development and formation by the Latin, Germanic, Celtic and Nordic peoples. From ancient Greece is derived the philosophical and epistemological elements and the foundations of education and of ethics and aesthetics; from Rome the elements of law and statecraft and government; from Judaism and Christianity the elements of religious faith; and from the Latin, Germanic, Celtic and Nordic peoples their independent and national spirit and traditional values, and the development and advancement of the natural and physical sciences and technology which they, together with the Slavic peoples, have pushed to such pinnacles of power. Islam too has made very significant contributions to Western civilization in the sphere of knowledge and in the inculcation of the rational and scientific spirit, but the knowledge and the rational and scientific spirit have been recast and remoulded to fit the crucible of Western culture so that they have become fused and amalgamated with all the other elements that form the character and personality of Western civilization. But the fusion and amalgamation thus evolved produced a characteristic dualism in the world-view and values of Western culture and civilization; a dualism that cannot be resolved into a harmonious unity, for it is formed of conflicting ideas, values, cultures, beliefs, philosophies, dogmas, doctrines and theologies altogether reflecting an all-pervasive dualistic vision of reality and truth locked in despairing combat. Dualism abides in all aspects of Western life and philosophy: the speculative, the social, the political, the cultural – just as it pervades with equal inexorableness the Western religion.

It formulates its vision of truth and reality not upon revealed knowledge and religious belief, but rather upon cultural tradition reinforced by strictly philosophical premises based upon speculations pertaining mainly to secular great store upon man as physical entity and rational animal, setting great store upon man's intellectual capacity along to unravel the mysteries of his total environment and involvement in existence, and to conceive out of the results of speculations based upon such premises his evolutionary ethical and moral values to guide and order his life accordingly. There can be no certainty in philosophical speculations in the sense of religious certainty based on revealed knowledge understood and experienced in Islam; and because of this the knowledge and values that project the world-view and direct the life of such a civilization are subject to constant review and change.

Reliance upon the powers of the human intellect alone to guide man through life; adherence to the validity of the dualistic vision of reality and truth; affirmation of the reality of the evanescent-aspect of existence projecting a secular world-view; espousal of the doctrine of humanism; emulation of the allegedly universal reality of drama and tragedy in the spiritual, or transcendental, or inner life of man, making drama and tragedy real and dominant elements in human nature and existence – these elements altogether taken as a whole are, in my opinion, what constitute the substance, the spirit, the character and personality of Western culture and civilization. It is these elements that determine for that culture and civilization the moulding of its concept of knowledge and the direction of its purpose, the formation of its contents and the systematization of its dissemination; so that the knowledge that is now systematically disseminated throughout the world is not necessarily *true* knowledge, but that which is imbued with the character and personality of Western culture and civilization, and charged with its spirit and geared to its purpose. And it is these elements, then, that must be identified and separated and isolated from the body of knowledge, so that knowledge may be distinguished from what is imbued with these elements, for these elements and what is

19

imbued with them do not represent knowledge as such but they only determine the characteristic form in which knowledge is conceived and evaluated and interpreted in accordance with the purpose aligned to the world-view of Western civilization. It follows too that apart from the identification and separation and isolation of these elements from the body of knowledge, which will no doubt also alter the conceptual form and values and interpretation of some of the contents of knowledge as it is now presented, its very purpose and system of deployment and dissemination in institutions of learning and in the domain of education must needs be altered accordingly. It may be argued that what is suggested is but *another, alternative* interpretation of knowledge imbued with other conceptual forms and values aligned to another purpose which reflects another world-view; and that this being so, and by the same token, what is formulated and disseminated as knowledge might not necessarily reflect *true* knowledge. This, however, remains to be seen, for the test of true knowledge is in man himself, in that if, through an alternative interpretation of knowledge man knows himself and his ultimate destiny, and in thus knowing he achieves happiness, then that knowledge, in spite of its being imbued with certain elements that determine the characteristic form in which it is conceived and evaluated and interpreted in accordance with the purpose aligned to a particular world-view, is true knowledge; for such knowledge has fulfilled man's purpose for knowing.

(ii) *Psychological and moral crisis and Muslim youth*
     Maulana Abul Hasan Ali Nadwi: from *Education in Saudi Arabia*

Maulana Abul Hasan Ali Nadwi, Rector of Nadwatul Ulema of Lucknow, India, a well-known seat of traditional Islamic learning, is a scholar of repute and a writer of many profound and significant works on Islam and its role in the modern world. In the following extract he analyses the impact of anti-religious forces on society and especially on Muslim Youth.

(1) In a society passing through a psychological and moral crisis, produced by an hysterical wave of materialism, where wealth and not morality is the standard of honour and respect, no educational system, however developed and widespread, can fructify and give rise to a spiritual-moral society. Educated classes and even teachers and thinkers occupying important positions in the universities are swept away by the strong current of materialism; they become like small pieces of minced meat put in the salt which quickly dissolve in it. It would therefore, not at all be desirable to close one's eyes to

the strong materialistic tidal wave inundating everything that stands in its way. It becomes imperative, in the circumstances, to give more serious thought to these maladies which are making the Muslim nation weak and infirm. The only way to combat this evil is to make arrangements for the widest possible dissemination of the Islamic *Dawah*, the spiritual-moral teachings of Islam through good healthy literature and journals propagating ethical norms and the awe of God in public dealings. If necessary, laws should be enacted for the purpose and those found offending these rules of conduct should be punished.

(2) There is a need to present personal examples of moderation, simplicity, selflessness, readiness to serve one's country and seeking one's recompense only from God Almighty. We all know that personal and ennobling examples set by individuals have a great psychological effect on all sections of people of every age and country. They once produced a spirit of piety and devotion which gave birth to the greatest 'ulama savants and revivalists of faith in earlier generations. These savants and scholars devoted their lives to the service of learning and moral and religious reform without the least expectation of any material return. Some of these leading spirits of olden times have left indelible marks of their intellectual attainments; often they even moulded the course of history. But the products of our universities and other higher seats of learning nowadays find themselves swept away by the general current of the time unmindful of everything else except a better and prosperous future for themselves. They are all suffering from a common disease which we can call 'careerism'.

(3) The publicity media are, in every country, more potent and extensive than the educational system. Being almost as freely available as air and water in so-called civilized and developed countries, no one can avoid them. In setting standards and values, in appraisal and evaluation of material things and ideas and in changing the predispositions of people they play such a vital role that publicity experts have come to regard them as the heart of man.

Lack of complete coordination between these powerful and widespread means of publicity and education have given rise to conflict and confusion, mental unrest and chaos in Muslim young men. The conditions obtaining today in Muslim lands have made the work of our educationists and reformers all the more difficult and they are very often dejected in regard to the futility of their endeavours.

Now, if you permit me, I would like to quote what I said in a seminar of Muslim Youths, held in an important Arab country, in reply to a question about the reasons for present perplexity and discomfiture found in young people.

'A Muslim youth is passing through a state of disconcerning bewilderment and a dilemma. He is guided by the press and publicity media like radio and television. He listens to talks and programmes which more often obliterate whatever feeble traces of Islamic education and training are left in him and thus expose him to an intellectual vagueness and psychological frustration. The modern press, deemed respectable by the majority, provides him with inflammatory, sensational and irresponsible material. The sexy pictures and lascivious headlines which attract his attention first, incite his lust and create doubts in his mind about the norms of morality and absolute truths. Then, he reads books written by experts whom he considers to be authorities on their subjects, and they create uncertainties about his ethical creed and faith, give rise to doubts about the sources of Islamic history and Sharia and make him sceptical even about the value of his own language and literature. There is an intellectual confrontation ending in uncertainty and doubt about the imperishable nature of his own moral code and convictions, the competence and potentiality of his people, and the value of his own ideas, ideals and language. He is persuaded to place reliance on a jumble of seemingly attractive ideas and so he is laid open to intellectual confusion and bewilderment. All these are sufficient to confound even a mature and rightminded person. How then, can young and immature minds be expected to withstand such a strong current of scepticism?'

Literature produced in the bigger Arab cities, at least during the past fifty years, is providing intellectual guidance to the younger generation but it has sown the seeds of uncertainty and doubt in the minds of its readers. Now the young have begun to disdain their own past and future – even their own existence and that of proven facts and realities. This is the literature which is produced for earning easy money, fame, cheap popularity, or even simply for worthless slogans.

It is a literature which has served no purpose except to open the doors of mental discontent and disbelief. Radio and television transmissions compound the situation; they are seductive and lacking in any healthy or pre-determined objective and they appeal to the baser instincts of sensuality. These have all combined to create an extremely difficult problem for all right-thinking persons, in both the East and West. The corrupting influences I have just mentioned have made our youth indolent and worldly. They avoid any task that needs perseverance and hard labour. This state of affairs has led a number of educationists and psychologists to acknowledge the fact that the present attitude of mind in the young has given rise to a predisposition to attempt dangerous hazards merely for the sake of novelty and often without regard for life and property. Teachers and guardians exercise little control over students while academic and cultural standards are going down because radio and television transmissions are claiming a greater part of students' time and leaving very little time for their studies. This is a problem that needs serious examination to find a solution that must not be deferred much longer without disastrous consequences.

(4) There is yet another danger. The Education Ministries of our Arab and Muslim countries have begun sending young and immature students to Europe and America for higher studies without giving the least thought to the intellectual maturity and spiritual and moral development of these students. Many of these students are actually sent abroad while they are still in adolescence – an age most crucial and precarious for shaping the future course of their lives. Sending these students to countries where moral corruption has spread like an infectious disease, where the higher and nobler values of life have been uprooted and where teachers and guardians have failed to exercise any control over their wards and students, amounts to playing with the lives of our next generation. In due course, these students will be teachers in their own countries. If we expect that these students will absorb Western learning and the better aspects of Western civilization but will keep aloof from its corrupting influences, we are living in a fools' paradise. It is against Nature, particularly as these students usually have to stay as paying guests with European or American families in the absence of any separate boarding houses with an Islamic atmosphere to sustain them intellectually, morally and spiritually. The action of these Education Ministries is tantamount to throwing these students in a river after tying their hands and feet, and then expecting them to swim across the river safe and dry.

(5) The problem of girls' education is no less important; it is rather more delicate and crucial. It demands greater thought and a firmer determination to solve the problem. The imitative pattern of girls' education, accepted by the East and West, in certain peculiar circumstances obtaining today, is ill-conceived and demands an entirely new and different approach. It requires to be planned afresh with courage and intelligence. The history of nations bears witness to the fact that the

greatest single factor in reducing great nations to a state of cultural enfeeblement and moral anarchy and, then, to their ultimate disintegration, has been the breakdown of the institution of the family. Avoidance of household responsibilities by womenfolk, and shameless make-up and beauty treatment, are the surest signs of pagan *ignorance*. Wherever we see a nation sinking in decline and decay, we also see its womenfolk refusing to remain at home, to do their work, to keep house and bear and bring up children. Instead of making her home a refuge and a place of rest for her husband, she tries to shoulder responsibilities in farms and factories, in offices and workshops and wants to outdo him at his own work. Western society has brought this calamity on itself, the structure of its family system has become topsy-turvey, its social framework has crumbled and its family structure, which used to be the breeding place of its younger generation and the reservoir of its power, and which helped it to gain ascendancy over other nations, has been broken up. Western sociologists are now summoning up courage to acknowledge their mistake, but having lost control are beginning to succumb to a sense of despondency about the ultimate doom of their civilization.

Any thoughtless reproduction of this unsuccessful system of education in any Muslim country, especially in Saudi Arabia, the centre and strong-hold of Islam, would be too dangerous for its safety as well as for the preservation of its identity and the message it has for the world. We should take a lesson from the experiences of Western peoples and try to avoid the dangers confronting them.

(iii) *Brainwashing by mass-media and resistance to Islamicization by the Westernized elitist class*
   Syed Altaf Gauhar: from *Education and the Mass Communication Media*

Syed Altaf Gauhar, at one time Communications Secretary of the Pakistan Government and, later, editor of the influential English daily, *Dawn*, and recently, Chief editor of publications of the Islamic Council of Europe, discusses how the elitist group which is controlling power in Muslim countries has been brainwashed by Western secular education system and how the mass-media introduced and controlled by this group show the influence of the master-mind of Western editors from whom ideas and even programmes are borrowed.

I have tried to make two points: (1) it is the editorial mind, governed by its own interests and objectives, which determines the presentation and interpretation of ideas and events, and (2) while the editorial mind has some awareness of a passive national audience, we in the Muslim

World represent an irrelevant audience to the mass media, controlled by the industrialized West or the Communist countries. I am using the word 'irrelevant' for a particular purpose – not to suggest that the contact is accidental or superfluous, but to emphasize is the total incompatibility of the interests and objectives of the Muslim audience with the interests and objectives of the present controllers of mass media. It is this factor of irrelevance which makes us a particularly easy target to attack. Since the interests, values and objectives of this audience have no relevance for the controllers of mass media, they can destroy them without any sense of loss or risk of retaliation. To summarize, it is no longer possible to keep the institutions of education and the mass media of communications in separate compartments: the two have to be integrated.

In the reconstruction of the system of education in the Muslim World, it is the Muslim mind which should determine not only its methods of teaching and training, its courses of study and procedures of evaluation, but also the policy and operations of the mass media of communications including newspapers, newsagencies, radio broadcasts, television programmes, films and other audio-visual facilities. I think that it should be possible for all the Muslim countries to train their own nationals, in no more than three to five years, in all branches of mass communication media. The real need is to have the right attitude towards the media. It consists of a set of technical instruments in which you must learn to control and employ in the service of your people. It would make no sense to reject technical instruments as obnoxious or vile – to do so would be to reject gun-powder for self-defence, or aircraft for travel. But to use a new instrument one has to acquire a new discipline. If one wants to get the best results from a camera one should develop an eye to look at objects through the lens. To use a microphone, one must learn to speak at a level, and from a distance which would not distort the frequencies. For an imaginative and effective use of the screen, one should learn the theory and technique of employing sound and colour to produce a coherent picture. A producer or a teacher who uses slides, canned programmes or videotape must know how to operate the equipment. If he is unable to adjust the picture on the screen, his students are not likely to be impressed by his knowledge of the theory of television. In this and allied matters full use should be made of technical training facilities provided by the industrialized countries but always under national supervision. When it comes to the designing and production of educational or informational programmes, we must have our own people at all levels who can exercise judgement and independence in developing them, from the beginning to the end, in accordance with our values, our cultural needs and our objectives.

(iv) *Muslim minorities in the West: conflict between home-traditions and a secular environment*
Dr. Muhammad Anwar: from *Young Muslims in a multi-cultural society: educational needs and policy implications*

Dr. Muhammad Anwar, at one time a member of the Community Relations Commission and at present a Senior Executive Officer in the Research Section at the Commission for Racial Equality discusses the condition of the younger generation of Muslims in Great Britain and stresses the importance of the role of education in the preservation and furtherance of Islamic values.

In a minority-dominant group approach, the ideology behind the concepts of 'assimilation', 'absorption' or 'integration' reflect the ideology of the dominant group and, therefore, any group which remains unabsorbed, or not assimilated, is usually considered to upset the equalization of social relations in the society. On the other hand, ethnic minorities interpret the concept of integration to mean the acceptance by the majority of their separate ethnic identity. Sociologists reflect these two viewpoints by using the concept of 'pluralistic integration' where a group continues to maintain itself as a unit on its own, but is nevertheless accepted by the majority as part of the society.

This means that a group such as Muslims, integrated in this sense, would keep its own distinguishing features such as religion, language, family patterns but its children would go to state schools and its members would do work with the majority. Religion is an important and sensitive part of a group's ethnic identity and the religious needs of the Muslims in Britain are very important in this regard. These needs are related to worship, burial, education, family laws, etc. The lack of facilities to practise Islam in Britain has been pointed out in relation to school uniforms, single-sex state schools, difficulties of worship and burial etc. This list is by no means exhaustive, rather is it indicative of the problems faced by Muslims in a Western country where the environment is non-Islamic and unsympathetic.

These needs are significant for the second generation members born and brought up in a different cultural environment from that of the first generation migrants, experiencing tensions between minority-majority culture. Therefore, what is required is not only the changes envisaged in the Race Relations Act, but changes in government policy generally,

26

with regard to the needs of Muslims (and other religious groups) in terms of creating understanding and positive policies on resources, reallocation and changed codes for professionals. It appears that there is willingness among Muslims (and other Asian religious groups) in Britain to adapt to the social structure of this country without losing their identity as Muslims. Muslims seem to fulfil Eisenstadt's requirements for a 'balanced' ethnic group in a pluralistic society. As a community, they have become a part of the social structure of the new society, although individual members have not completely changed cultures. Muslims constitute an ideologically oriented community and are supposed to conform to certain moral and spiritual principles of Islam enunciated in the Holy Quran and the traditions of the Prophet Muhammad (peace be upon him). This does not mean that in order to keep this balance, they are not facing any problems. We have to take into account certain difficulties which arise in relation to the practice of their beliefs, their self-identity as Muslims in society where they are likely to experience feelings of rejection and hostility associated with belonging to a minority group in an unsympathetic environment. In addition, they enjoy no protection in law against discrimination on the basis of religion.

Young Muslims who are constantly exposed to the dominant society's culture take various aspects of Islam less seriously than they ought to. One of the reasons for this change is the lack of proper public and community facilities for Muslims to transmit regularly religious behaviour, beliefs and experiences to the young generation in the same way as parents would do in a Muslim country. Many Muslim parents express distress at the permissiveness of young people in British society. This increases their worry about the moral socialization of their children at school.

The results of our research demonstrates the conditions (eg. lack of religious education in schools) under which people practise religion and their attitudes in general. Those who wish to promote religion must change these situations, for young Muslims in particular.

The Muslim situation as a whole fits into the social learning theory which states that religious behaviour, beliefs and experiences are simply part of culture, and are regularly transmitted from generation to generation in the same way as any other custom. This view has been widely held and there is much evidence to show that children reared in different parts of the world tend to acquire, if unchecked, the local religious beliefs and the values. The environmental factors and attitudes discussed above provide evidence of this happening in Britain.

Religious beliefs and attitudes are modified by membership of educational and other social groups. It is thus apparent that the communication of values through education often results in conflict with values that the Muslim children learn at home and in their community. Also for Muslims, culture, language, family relations and religion are intimately linked and, therefore, changes are seen to be necessary in religious education in schools and other related practices.

Religious leaders and parents feel very strongly that aspects related to their own religion should be taught in school to all children. In this way, they believe mutual understanding and respect will be increased. This suggestion is in line with the accepted public policy in Britain of 'cultural diversity in an atmosphere of mutual tolerance'.

2. Religion in Education: Confusion of its Role

(i) *Impact of anti-religious ideas and confusion of values*
   Muhammad Qutb: from *The Role of Religion in Education*

Muhammad Qutb, Professor of Islamic Studies and Comparative Religion, King Abdulzaziz University, Mecca, is a member of the Muslim Brotherhood and an advocate of a return to the pristine purity of Islam. His most popular book that has been translated into modern languages is *Islam, the Misunderstood Religion*. He writes in Arabic, but his influence has spread all over the Muslim world.

We, in most parts of the Muslim world, do not resort to the Sharia nor do our life-governing laws draw upon it. Our lives, on the whole, are not patterned to Allah's Curriculum which comprises belief, duties of worship, work, feeling, conduct, politics, economics, sociology, etc; in fact it encompasses life and the hereafter in one self-contained discipline. But our concepts and approaches, or feelings and thoughts, our morals and modes of behaviour are not derived from Islam. The vast majority of these have reached us from every corner of the world where Islam is unknown and not believed in. Religion, as we feel and approach it now, has dwindled from its integrated inclusiveness known to earlier Muslim generations into something more or less akin to the Western ecclesiastical approach, namely, an emotional relationship between Lord and servant outside the sphere of actual life. This, which we ought to acknowledge quite frankly and unequivocally if we are to deal with our subject honestly and seriously, casts its impenetrable shadow over our entire lives; besides, it is closely relevant to education curricula. . . .

To make Allah's doctrine rule supreme is, in itself, a sound educational proposal to which the entire human race should contribute. Saying one's prayers at their appointed times is extremely educative. Consolidating and intensifying Islamic patterns of conduct among children would help them retain Islamic morals and education in later life. The sight of God-fearing women wholly committed to the divine word of Allah, or a man taking his words, steps, work and duties of worship seriously, is a type of education which leaves its indelible mark on children's behaviour. . . .

It is undeniable that our hold on religion has now weakened. Religion has gradually been banished from our minds and hearts. The home and the environment instead of promoting religious education, have contrarily combined to undermine it. In such conditions only school curricula remain as channels of information through which religious education can be promoted and intensified. In such a situation, a lesson given in the classroom of the mosque cannot be sufficient nor can a lesson crammed with rigid disconnected bits of information put together the way it was devised and planned centuries ago. And do the information media welcome a sermon or a religious speech? The formal lesson, the sermon and the religious speech exist more or less like a fine building that was once magnificent but is now in ruins. It has collapsed, leaving behind a few stones to remind us of the gigantic walls that had once stood. Will those stones help re-build the fine gigantic structure that was once erected?

In fact the picture is far worse than that. To summarize what has been mentioned so far, since educational institutions gave up their role and the entire burden of religious education has been lodged in the educational curricula and the media of information, the formal lesson on religion, the sermon or the religious address has proved utterly insufficient and futile for religious education. What wonder then if the atmosphere of a formal lesson at school, or a sermon or a religious speech on radio and T.V. is far from being religious and is very often irreligious? It will soon be discovered that the subject material taught and the teaching methods used are not very dissimilar from those of the Western world, i.e., a world absolutely anti-religious though it hides its anti-religious nature behind the curtain of secularism and claims that it is only non-religious and not anti-religious.

(ii) *Loss of 'all-inclusive-togetherness' through multiplicity of systems without a common goal*
A. K. Brohi: from *Role of National Education in an Ideological State*

A. K. Brohi, a philosopher by training and an advocate by profession, is a modern Muslim thinker of Pakistan with a deep spiritual commitment to both the mystical and the practical aspects of life. He has held various governmental positions, once being the Law Minister of Pakistan and then the High Commissioner for Pakistan in India, and is currently holding the post of Minister for Religion and Law. He has several books on philosophy and Islam to his credit. He believes in an 'all-inclusive-togetherness' in education, and integration that would truly reflect the all-comprehensiveness of Islam.

The fostering of a sound religious belief, I submit, is the main task of Education. Unfortunately education in our times is often described as either being *religious* or *non-religious* (i.e., *secular*) that is to say, education that teaches elements of theology and religious law and education that teaches how to qualify for liberal callings like that of the law, medicine or engineering. These are supposed to be *two different kinds of Education*. In the last category comes education in sciences and in arts which are taught in our schools, in our colleges and in our universities. But I, for one, do not see how education can be so artificially divided; all education is an attempt to *cultivate the soil of an individual's life*, to kindle the Divine Spark that is lying buried in all of us. If Education does minister to that sacred flame and make it glow with light, well and good, but if it does not, in my reckoning it does not merit the name of education, no matter what else it is able to do. The Human Mind is impressionable at all ages and it is the task of Education to see that it remains impressionable right to the end of life. Education is thus education for life. It enables the best in us to be brought forth, to be nurtured and advanced. It imparts to us the awareness of our real place in the scheme of things. The extent to which we have learnt to discipline ourselves in the historical present in order that our dormant faculties blossom and qualify us for the rewards of higher life, is precisely the extent to which we have been educated.

It is true there is a certain type of education which prepares us to tackle what may be called the practical tasks of life; here the aim is to teach certain technical skills in order that students can gainfully employ themselves for the purposes of earning their livelihood. But what is contended is, that even this sort of discipline, if it is not geared to the basic purpose of highlighting the best of which we, as human beings, are capable, is not worth much and certainly cannot be regarded as the final consummation of the educational process. Similar remarks apply to the artificial distinctions that are often drawn between education being *personal* and *social*, or between *self-education* and education required from *external agencies*, or between the education of the *mind* and education of the *body*, or between the *education of the intellect* and the *education of emotions and the will*. All these artificial partition walls that are often erected to set forth the terrains of various types of education hardly do justice to the overall purpose of education. The whole of the educational process which as shown above, is as large as life itself and traverses the whole gamut of human civilization and culture, has for its aim the development of the individual and of the society of which he is a member. Similarly the distinction between professional education and education in humanities (or what is also called general education), although useful to pinpoint the specific goals they are designed to reach – the former helping the student to qualify for handling some profession and the latter to secure his development as a human being – is in fact an artificial distinction in the sense that the overall and real meaning of education is thereby blurred.

Curricula are often divided into 'arts' and 'sciences' and these in their turn into various sub-branches, to say nothing of subject areas such as history, philosophy and literature. This division serves a useful purpose in that it enables students to specialize in a particular sphere of knowledge. But then an attempt should also be made to fix the student's attention on that 'All-inclusive-togetherness of things which is both the first step of naivete and the last step of sophistication'. The student's objective is that dimly outlined and exhaustible immensity which is called 'the universe' or 'the world'. Here we are reminded of the wise saying of a Roman Philosopher who remarked, 'Since I am human, there is nothing human which is outside the range of my concern and study.'

We must enable our students not only to be well informed in the sense that they are made aware of the inheritance which has been bequeathed them by the human race, but they themselves must be drilled into becoming the serviceable agents who can impart a new direction or creative impulse to history. And this they can do, if they are helped to form correct judgements in relation to suitable selected data submitted for their consideration. It is no use acquiring an encyclopaedic mind if that mind at the same time is so stunted in its growth that it cannot form a correct judgement on even elementary matters.

3. Educational Remedy

(i) *A common integrated system with Islamic schools of thought in all branches of knowledge is the first priority*
First World Conference on Muslim Education, 1977: *Conference Book*, pp. 12–13

The education system that the Muslim countries have imported from the West for the sake of improving their own instruments of civilization is serving their material aim. It is giving the Muslims the knowledge that is helping them to achieve technological progress. But it is at the same time creating in their minds the same doubts and confusion, the same disintegration of human personality and hence of values which the West is suffering from. Unless Muslim scholars get together to create their own schools of Social Sciences and Humanities and rise to challenge the hypothesizing of western scientists who ignore the operation of the Divine Will in Nature, the time is not far off when Muslim societies will be as 'permissive' as Western societies are and Islam will be safely preserved only in book-form in the Quran and the Hadith.

It is true that this may not come too easily because there is still a traditional system of education and there are groups of people who adhere to that system. But the present system has given rise to secularized pressure-groups and these groups are fast capturing power from the more religious-minded people. There is thus some tension and conflict between the secular and the religious groups. This conflict has already expressed itself openly in Turkey, Egypt, Indonesia, Iraq, Syria and Pakistan, and led to internal disunity and even bloodshed. This can be avoided only if Islamic schools of thought in all spheres of knowledge can replace Western schools of thought and show that the Islamic schools of thought through their integration of the Body and Spirit, Matter and Mind, Temporary and Eternal, the so-called 'Secular' and the 'Divine' can and do succeed in bringing about socio-economic progress towards peace and harmony, economic prosperity and political progress. The challenge is a mammoth one and demands nothing less than a Jihad – an educational Jihad – to meet and overcome it.

(ii) *Integration of education and society by looking at the harmony achieved by Islamic education in the past and by drawing lessons from them and thus recreating true Islamic education.*

Dr. Zaki Badawi from: *Traditional Islamic Education: Its Aims and Purposes*

Dr. Zaki Badawi who was for a long time Dean of the Faculty of Islamic Studies at Ahmadu Bello University of Nigeria and is at present the Director of the Islamic Culture Centre of London, gives an interpretation of the traditional Islamic system and compares it with the modern system and indicates the methods by which the traditional system may become the source of solving all problems of social disorder and imbalances.

Traditional Muslim education was not an activity separated from other aspects of society. It acted in harmony with all other activities and institutions to confirm them and to be reinforced by them. Not surprisingly the mosque, the heart of all religious activities, was the apex of the whole system. Neither the educator nor the student was isolated from the rest of the community. They more often than not combined other functions with that of education, thus retaining their close contact with everyday life. There was always a close personal relationship between the teacher and the student which ensured that moral and spiritual guidance was given alongside the teaching of various skills.

Success was of course important but failure did not turn the individual into a useless burden on society. Whatever he had learnt, and however little, would still be of value and his place within society would still be guaranteed.

The community of Muslims is founded upon a creed and the constant values of a firm faith which gives its members their distinctive character and unmistakable Islamic personality. Yet, even if Muslims of today have waxed dense and shown an earth-bound proclivity, Islam remains true to itself and retains its perennial quality which lies in waiting for some inspired group of believers who can give the deathless ethos a new lease of vigorous renewal in this world. Therefore the work of the curriculum in the Muslim community cannot be limited to catering for this brief life. It must look forward and upwards to life in the Here-after. This outlook is given in a nutshell by the following quotation from the Quran : 'But seek amidst that which Allah has given thee, the Last Abode, and forget not thy portion of the present world : [Al-Qassas (the story) 77].

Thus the teacher in our Muslim context is no mere member of the school community. On the contrary, he has authority which springs from his strong personality for he follows in the trail of our first educator, Muhammad (*Sallallahu alaihi wasallam*): 'Now there has come to you a Messenger from among yourselves; grievous to him is your suffering; anxious is he over you, gentle to the believers, compassionate' (Al-Taubah, i.e., Repentance – V.128).

The Muslim teacher is afraid normally lest his pupils should lapse into Jahiliya, i.e., the ignorance which Islam had superseded once and for all. He tries to ward off from them the evils of perversity and aberration. He is expected to do his utmost to impress upon the minds of his pupils the general ethos and the morality of Islam at the social and individual levels. This indeed is the positive role assigned by Islam to the teacher who is considered, thereby, to be a moral tutor. The teacher's authority is that of imparting useful knowledge to his pupils, after he has done his best to purify that from any defiling admixture of imported science which may disagree with the outlook of Islam. He, i.e., the teacher, is endowed with another kind of authority, which is that of moral mentor and guide *in loco parentis* to the pupils under his care.

The Muslim teacher must never detach himself from social issues which confront the people of his community. His can never be a passive or indifferent attitude towards the problems of the community of their solution. His success is measured by both the matter presented and the spiritual lesson, not only to the cerebral part of the personality of the pupil, but to the whole and integrated human personality in him.

When wisely vetted and sagaciously selected syllabi meet with the right kind of responsible and responsive teacher, who can carry over both the matter and the spirit of what he teaches to his class, then one can say that a proper breeding environment is now ready to impart to the pupil true religious orientations within a fully live community. The net result of producing men of moral and civic integrity who have perceptive, critical and perspicacious judgement should then be no mere mirage before our vision.

But the final product is no mere philosophical onlooker but an active, knowledgeable and effective citizen with a fruitful occupation in the community. He or she should be an alert and mentally agile human being who is always ready to act sensibly and appositely with regard to the rapidly changing social scene. Training in the mosque university was a combined activity in which both student and teacher took part. The student had to be persuaded rather than instructed and the teacher had to argue his case rather than dictate it. In this way the personality and the intellectual ability of the student was allowed to develop and grow.

Unlike the modern system which operates like a factory with a production line measuring its success by statistical tables, traditional Islamic education measured its activity by the fact that it stimulated the community as a whole to take an interest in the higher issues so fundamental to its nature and survival.

Because of his role in the community and in the field of education the teacher acted not simply as the guide to better knowledge but also as the example to better conduct. Teaching was not simply a profession to be sold but a role to be fully and completely performed.

In all this it can be seen that the school reflected most faithfully the society.

(iii) *Society needs leaders trained in Islamic values but educated to meet the needs of the modern society*
    Dr. Basheer Tom: from *Education and Society*

Dr. Basheer Tom, Assistant Professor in the Department of Education, King Abdulaziz University, Mecca, while discussing the relation between education and society accepts John Dewey's idea that education must answer to society's needs but rejects his concept that the school should reflect life. According to Islam, he says, the school should transmit from generation to generation perennial values and thus provide leadership to society.

It is essential that our education should prepare us to understand our rapidly changing environment of inventions and techniques. For ours is a world dominated by the artefact of technology and also by rapid social change. Manual dexterity and mental alertness and self-reliance are indispensable prerequisities for dealing with this environment. The phenomena of the constant influx of people into cities and the era of the megalopolis with its host of technicians and experts and the rat race for daily bread are permanent features of our contemporary world.

Chapter Two

Aims and Objectives of Islamic Education

Islamic Education and the Concept of Man

Education, shorn of all frills and furbelows, signifies the transmission of experience from one generation to another. What is transmitted in an organized society with a history is not individual experience as such but the cumulative experience of past generations enshrined in folklore, traditions, customs, poetry and the like. These in their turn crystallize around – and also mirror – the basic concept of the place of man in this universe that a society has developed and cherishes. This is as true of Islamic society as of the West.[1]

The real nature of a system of education and its difference from other systems can be understood properly only when the concept of man underlying it is analysed and examined. In what respects then does the Islamic concept of man differ from other concepts and to what extent is it mirrored in the system of education that we call Islamic?

The first thing worth bearing in mind is that Islam subscribes to no theory of original sin;[2] it does not believe that man has a basically tainted nature and spends the whole of his life struggling against it. The story of the Fall of Adam is part of the common heritage of Islam and Christianity, but Islam does not interpret it to mean that corruption and evil are inherent in Adam's descendants. On the contrary, Islam emphasizes that every child, like his primordial grandfather, is born in a state of innocence and if it succumbs to evil later, it is because of its failure to rise above temptation. But for every one man who yields to temptation, there are scores who do not, a fact which points to man's capacity for good.

It is no accident that time and again in the Quran man is described as Allah's vicegerent, as the crown and chief of His creation.[3] Intelligence and knowledge[4] are spoken of as His greatest gifts – received from God – which he is called upon to utilize in the service of his Maker. These gifts and the tremendous power they confer on him render him accountable to God for all his actions, for the important as well as the unimportant ones: indeed the distinction which he might wish to make between the two is illusory; he will be held responsible for every detail of his life, for the manner in which he employed his gifts and the use to which he put his intelligence and knowledge.

Now, this conception of man's responsibility shows education in an Islamic society to be an activity unlike any other, either within its limits or in any other society. It is assumed to have unlimited potentialities in the matter of moulding character and elevating man to the highest rank in God's creation of which he is capable. Islam does not believe that some children are doomed by reason of their birth and race to exist at the level of beasts whilst some others, again by virtue of their birth and race, are predisposed to excellence. Born without any inherent handicaps – genetic or racial – they attain or fail to attain a full flowering of their faculties according as their parents or their society educates them.[5]

Aims of Education

But what are they expected to receive from a process of education? The content of education which as we have said earlier means the transference of experience, can be divided for a Muslim into two categories: experience in the form of skills or technical knowledge whose nature varies from age to age and which is bound to change constantly; and experience based on certain constant or permanent values embodied in religion and scripture. These latter consist of those eternal verities which are not subject to change, and which for a Muslim are defined in the Quran and Sunnah in the clearest possible terms.

The system of education which has been characteristic of Muslim society down the ages, whether it was what the West calls liberal education or technical education (Islam recognizes no distinction between the two as regards the problem of values), has always attempted to uphold the premises referred to above. The essential goodness of human nature, man's accountability, his commitment to a set of God-given primordial values – these formed the foundation of whatever education a Muslim youth received. The result, it has been rightly claimed, was the growth of a society in which different generations and occupations and strata lived in harmony with one another, bound together by a common faith.

Believing as it does that the true aim of education is to produce men who have faith as well as knowledge, the one sustaining the other, Islam does not think that the pursuit of knowledge by itself without reference to the spiritual goal that man must try to attain, can do humanity much good. Knowledge divorced from faith is not only partial knowledge, it can even be described as a kind of new ignorance. The man who has lost his faith in God is not recognized by Islam as a man whose knowledge can be described as deep. Such a person, however extensive his acquaintance with books, has but acquired only a fragmentary view of the universe.

What is more important from Islam's point of view is that he may sooner or later find himself committed to courses of action which are bound to be immoral, unethical and socially dangerous because subversive of those laws which hold society together.

Islamic education consequently insists that piety and faith must be clearly recognized in syllabuses as an aim to be systematically pursued. The test of any syllabus must be whether it brings the learner nearer to an understanding of God and of the relation in which man stands to his Maker. The subject the learner studies may be any one of the numerous subjects that universities teach; it could be something other than the conventional. But in each case the test of its validity and effectiveness will be whether it fosters a deeper awareness of the Divine Presence in the universe. If it does not it should be clearly understood to be at variance with the Islamic notion of education.[6]

It is from this premise that insistence on the study of scripture as the first step in education springs. The word of God, properly studied, can be relied upon to strengthen the foundations of faith, and once this has happened, the learner can proceed to explore the world without fear of losing his spiritual bearings.

Thus what distinguishes the Islamic system of education from the modern Western system is the importance it attaches to faith and piety as one of its fundamental aims. In the West, the aim of education is spoken of as being to produce a good individual and a good citizen, both of which aims Islam can accept. But having secularized education completely, the West fails to indicate how in the absence of a set of moral values, either of those aims can be realized. Western society is today in danger of disintegrating. There is nothing to hold it together except state laws, and when the justice of the state laws is in question, moral anarchy and urban lawlessness are the response.

Secularization of Education in the West and its Impact on Muslim Society

The decay of Islamic civilization and the rise of the modern West have been marked by the acceptance of doubt and scepticism as the basis of intellectual advancement and the consequent rejection of most of the values which Islam cherished.

The West has to its credit great achievements in science and technology which have made terrestrial life safer and more comfortable. The aeroplane, the telephone, radio, television, computers – to mention a few things – each symbolizes an advance in material progress of which the ancients had no conception.[7] Yet this material progress – which is within reach of common people – is not matched by any spiritual development. On the contrary, spiritually man today is much less happy than his predecessor two hundred years ago. Disharmony and tension have ruined his mental peace, rendered his social life infernal, and deprived his existence of all meaning and purpose. The more the West reaches out for a solution without spiritual values and faith, the greater is the confusion, the greater the agony. Bizarre philosophies like existentialism and logical positivism try to discover a meaning in existence within the stuffy atmosphere of a Godless universe, but the more they seek to evade the central and crucial problem of faith, the more dreadfully thay fail to provide a satisfactory answer to the problems of life.[8]

But why, it may be asked, should this affect Muslim society? The answer to this question lies in a paradox.

Much as the Muslim, anchored in faith, disapproves of the spiritual nihilism of the West, he himself, because of his neglect of science and technology, has created around his society a suffocating atmosphere as oppressive as the spiritual sterility of the West. Want and poverty, disease and epidemic, colonialism and economic humiliation have forced him to realize that it is only by mastering science and technology that he can escape these problems. But when he turns to the West for his knowledge of science and technology, he finds that the whole of it is riddled with premises antithetical to his faith. Modern science and technology would lead him to banish God, to renounce faith, and to commit himself to the pursuit of mindless materialism.

The need for science and technology has, however, been so urgent for him that ever since he first became conscious of the disparity between himself and the Western world he has been desperately trying to master its secrets, copy its methods, emulate its examples, without waiting to consider the risks inherent in the process. The move towards the adoption of Western ideas began in the nineteenth century in many Muslim countries. The results which have manifested themselves in the course of the last fifteen decades or so have begun to frighten many Muslim thinkers. Are we, they ask, travelling the same path as has led to the purposelessness of the West?[9]

Modernization and Cultural Identity: the Process of Reconciliation

But how to avoid the risks without having to renounce modern knowledge? Can we discover a means of isolating the sterile values which have so warped Western life from the knowledge which they corrupt? Knowledge, Muslim scholars believe, cannot by itself be harmful or dangerous. It is the extraneous values and assumptions which man imparts into it which cause it to produce a spiritually harmful fall-out.

This is the nature of the crisis that Muslim societies which have embarked upon a programme of modernization face. They are anxious not to lose their identity, nor to lose their distinctive religious outlook, and not to be infected with Western spiritual diseases. In order to steer clear of these dangers they must scrutinize what they learn from the West and search in their text books for those basic assumptions which they cannot afford to accept except at their own peril.

Now for the purpose of isolating spurious values from real knowledge, Muslim scholars need to re-examine the commonly accepted Western classifications of knowledge in the light of the Islamic fundamentals. For no branch of knowledge, whether it is philosophy or physics, epistemology or economics, can be wholly divorced from underlying value-judgements. The differences between the pure sciences and the humanities is from this point of view a difference of degree. The scientist who declares himself a non-partisan observer of phenomena has to start from or rely on hypotheses, and these spring from sources saturated with non-scientific values. The Western world has been trying, at least since the birth of rationalism, to explain the universe without reference to God, and the assumption that it will eventually succeed in doing so has coloured all its findings. No Muslim could accept such an assumption. Consequently, the first task facing the Islamic world is to discover those hidden assumptions which have

40

little to do with science but which are mistaken for scientific truth by the unwary.

This task has not been undertaken in the recent past or where undertaken not performed with the thoroughness it demands. This is how the dual systems of education found in most Muslim countries arose. There was no duality of this kind in the heyday of Islam, when Muslims were in the van of scientific progress, and Muslim thinkers and philosophers set the pace for the world in all fields of knowledge. Having by their own neglect and backwardness allowed this position to change, they discovered painfully on waking up from their slothful slumber that advances had taken place under the leadership mainly of the West in science and technology which left them far behind. And when they sought to acquire the new science and technology and also the new advances in other areas of knowledge, they did so at first by superimposing the Western system of education on their own; but the two did not fit in with each other and were in consequence left to function independently. This worked to the disadvantage of the old, traditional system, and the tendency arose for a new generation, versed in the new knowledge of the West, but cut off from their own past, to grow alienated. This phenomenon has manifested itself in Pakistan, India, Bangladesh, Iran, Turkey, Egypt and all those other countries where Muslims tried to face the challenge of the West.

Patchwork solutions have been tried by combining traditional knowledge with courses in new subjects. But the combination does not work satisfactorily, for the values which inform the Western systems of education subtly penetrate the minds of our youth and throw them off their guard.[10]

This is how the need has arisen for a serious examination of the whole of basic knowledge, of the concept of man from which it derives and which it sustains. The true Islamic man – the *Insān Kamil* (The Perfect Man) – it is realized, is different in conception from man as conceived by the West.[11] Born in freedom, that is to say, without the handicap of original sin, this Islamic man never loses sight of his relation to his Maker, and education for him is an unfolding of those strengths and sensibilities which draw him nearer to God, inspire in him a consciousness of his obligations as the vicegerent of God, and teach him to treat the world as a great trust which must not be abused. He opposes such modern evils as abortion and vivisection, permissiveness and perversion, not on a consideration of the rights and wrongs of the issues in a given temporal context but on the grounds that they are contrary to God's injunctions. Freedom and bondage, justice and injustice, are matters which likewise are viewed by him *sub specie eternitatis*. The test he uses of the soundness of any educational system is whether it helps to kindle that spark of God-consciousness without which man remains a brute, and so judged, the system currently in vogue in the West, despite its manifold achievements is woefully deficient. It is to the removal of this deficiency in the light of Islam that we must bend our energies.

In the extracts that follow, a number of eminent contemporary Muslim scholars have discussed the aims of Islamic education and the concept of man which it mirrors from a number of points of view. They represent far-flung areas of the Muslim world, but what is remarkable is the unity of their outlook and the uniformity of the emphasis on the need for a new approach to the problem of education in the light of the fundamental concept which the Quran teaches. The *fons et origo* of Muslim thought is the Quran, and quite appropriately they have said time and again that no system of thought or education can be accept-able to Muslims whose tendency is to divert man from the highway of knowledge and wisdom which the Quran has charted for all time to come.

Extracts

1. To form the true Muslim

(i) Good and righteous man: Conference Book, pp. 76–78

The basic approach of 313 Muslim scholars who met at the First World Conference on Muslim Education held at Mecca in 1977 has been enunciated in the following paragraphs.

Concepts and attitudes

The aim of Muslim education is the creation of the 'good and righteous man' who worships Allah in the true sense of the term, builds up the structure of his earthly life according to the Shari'ah (law) and employs it to subserve his faith.

The meaning of worship in Islam is both extensive and comprehen-sive; it is not restricted to the physical performance of religious rituals only but embraces all aspects of activity: faith, thought, feeling, and work, in conformity with what Allah (Praise be to Him) says in the Holy Quran, 'I have created the Jinn and man only to worship Me' and

'Say, O my Lord, my prayers, my sacrifice, my life and my death are for Allah, the Lord of the Worlds Who hath no peer.'

Therefore, the foundation of civilization on this earth, the exploitation of the wealth, resources and energies that Allah has hidden in its bowels, the search for sustenance, the measures by which man can rise to full recognition of the ways of Allah in the Universe, knowledge of the properties of matter, and the ways in which they can be utilized in the service of faith and in the dissemination of the essence of Islam and in helping man to attain to a righteous and prosperous life – all these are considered forms of worship by which scholars and God-seekers come into closer contact with Allah. If such is the Islamic concept of worship, and if from the Islamic point of view the object of education in the most comprehensive sense of worship is the upbringing of the true believer, it follows that education must achieve two things. First, it must enable man to understand his Lord so that he worships Him in full conviction of His Oneness, observes the rituals, and abides by the Shari'ah and the Divine injunctions. Secondly, it must enable him to understand the ways of Allah in the universe, explore the earth, and use all that Allah has created to protect faith and reinforce His religion in the light of what Allah has said in the Quran,

'It is He who hath brought you from the earth and made you inhabit and inherit it.'

Thus the sciences of the Sharia (Islamic law) meet other sciences such as medicine, engineering, mathematics, psychology, sociology, etc., in that they are all Islamic sciences so long as they move within the framework of Islam and are in harmony with Islamic concepts and attitudes. All these sciences are necessary in reasonable degree, for the ordinary Muslim, while they are in a much more specialized form, required and sought by scholars, *mujtahidun* and jurists of the *Ummah* (the nation).

The Islamic concept of science does not impose any restriction or limitation on theoretical, empirical or applied sciences except for one limitation which pertains to the ultimate ends on the one hand and their actual effects on the other. In the Islamic sense science is a form of worship by which man is brought into closer contact with Allah; hence it should not be abused to corrupt faith and morals and to bring forth harm, corruption, injustice and aggression.

Consequently any science which is in conflict with faith and which does not serve its ends and requirements is in itself corrupt, and stands condemned and rejected and has no place in God's injunctions.

43

Every system of education embodies a particular philosophy which emanates from a particular concept from which it cannot be isolated. We cannot have a philosophy or an educational policy which is based on a concept not identical with the Islamic. This is what is now happening when we apply British, French, American or Russian policies of education because they, in the long run, conflict with and contradict the Islamic concept.

Islam embodies a general and comprehensive concept which sustains a self-contained, unique and distinctive educational policy. All we have to do is to base our education on this particular, unique and distinctive concept. When it comes to the means by which this end can be achieved, there is no objection whatsoever to the full exploitation of every successful human experiment so long as it is not in conflict with the Islamic concept.

The sources of knowledge, according to the Islamic concept, fall into two categories:

(1) Divine revelation where Allah teaches that man cannot, by himself, be rightly guided to the Divine truth and that life cannot be regulated in the proper manner in the absence of stable and unchangeable injunctions inspired by Allah, the Wise and the All-knowing whose knowledge encompasses all.

(2) The human intellect and its tools which are in constant interaction with the physical universe on the levels of observation, contemplation, experimentation and application. Man is free to do as he pleases subject to the condition that he remains fully committed to the Quran and the Sunnah.

Aims of education

Education should aim at the balanced growth of the total personality of Man through the training of Man's spirit, intellect, the rational self, feelings and bodily senses. Education should therefore cater for the growth of man in all its aspects: spiritual, intellectual, imaginative, physical, scientific, linguistic, both individually and collectively and motivate all these aspects towards goodness and the attainment of perfection. The ultimate aim of Muslim education lies in the realization of complete submission to Allah on the level of the individual, the community and humanity at large.

A training in values: both the absolute and the contingent
   Dr. A. M. Khusro: from *Education in the Islamic Society*

Dr. A. M. Khusro, Vice-Chancellor of Aligarh Muslim University, India, stresses the need to clarify the value system that should inform the reformed Islamic education system. Along with the inculcation and strengthening of basic values, the education system should also aim at training Muslim youth in the correct method of adjusting himself to a changing environment.

Every educational system worth the name must have a value system. The Islamic educational system must also clarify its value system. Every dynamic system has two essential features: (i) it has some unalterable, basic features which distinguish it from other systems; if these basic features disappear, the system disappears; (ii) it has a mechanism for changing the non-basic features; if such a mechanism for change does not exist, the system cannot adapt itself to changes in time and space and tends to stagnate and disappear.

The basic features of the Islamic constitution as embodied in the Quran and Sunnah are the *'nusus-e-qatai'* such as the belief in Allah, the faith in the Prophet and the basic attitude that all human activity is in the way of Allah. Those who do not believe in these are not Muslims. Islamic education has to inculcate these beliefs and attitudes in Muslim youth.

Side by side with the inculcation and strengthening of these basic values, Islamic education must build into the minds of Muslim youth a resilience, an adaptability and a mechanism for adjustment in worldly matters other than the fundamental beliefs. The Arabs were the first people to demonstrate such a resilience and adaptability during the heyday of Islamic intellectual effervescence. They acquired the Greek learning, subjected it to investigation, experimentation and expansion in such diverse fields as algebra, geometry, astronomy, navigation, chemistry and medicine and evolved the scientific principles of empiricism. The essence of empirical scientific attitude consisted of moving away form dogmatic beliefs and practices in worldly matters and raising healthy doubts about all propositions. By questioning everything that could be questioned, by asking at every step: 'is that so?' this empirical attitude gave immense freedom to human curiosity and became the cause of major scientific discoveries. Scientific beliefs came to be held tentatively rather than dogmatically, in the hope that further investigation and experimentation would lead to alternative beliefs. The Arabs carried this new empirical scientific attitude to Spain among other places and from there this attitude burst out into

Europe in the fifteenth and the sixteenth centuries and caused the Renaissance.

The Islamic education system must now adopt the same scientific empiricism in worldly matters which the Muslims had themselves invented but had forgotten during the past five centuries. The values of adaptability, experimentation, and tolerance (as opposed to dogma) must be embodied in the new system. This will, in all probability require the institution of *ijtihad* or interpretation of the Islamic law. *Ijtihad* must, of course, have the necessary safeguards: *ijtihad* cannot be resorted to in the matter of *nusus* or fundamentals; it cannot be used to destroy the spirit of Islam but only to further it; it cannot be undertaken by those who do not know the word of God and of the Prophet; nor can it be undertaken by those who do not know well the worldly institutions. As many of the learned men of the world do not know the word of God and the Prophet and many of the *'ulama* may not have had an exposure to the worldly institutions, a good Islamic educational system must open the doors of the Quran and Hadith to the men of religion. The new educational system must be an integrating force and must prepare men for *ijtihad* where it is due.

And finally, an Islamic educational system cannot be merely 'utilitarian' in character: it cannot only have career planning as its basic methodology. Utilitarianism has already led to such phenomenal problems as limitless consumerism, a mad race to acquire and consume more and more goods, with the consequent fouling and polluting of air and water, shortages of energy and exhaustion of exhaustible materials in the Western world. But while the sensitive among the western thinkers and educators have come to realize the 'sickness' of the West, it is a pity that many an Islamic country is thoughtlessly adopting the postures of the West and is indulging in ostentation, wasteful and un-Islamic consumption. Islamic education must correct these postures: it must teach the distinction between *halal* and *haram*, it must instil the values of self-restraint in consumption; it must promote the concepts of saving and investing, of economic justice and the redistribution of national income in Islamic countries.

These values have to be promoted not only in Islamic countries but also among Muslim minorities in other countries. For Muslim minorities in non-Muslim countries it is much better that the Governments of those countries are religiously neutral rather than committed to a religion which in that case is bound to be the religion of the majority. In a religiously neutral set-up the Muslims are relatively free to provide for themselves and their children Islamic values.

2. *Education for Wisdom (Hikmah): Need for Complete Reorientation Because of the Confusion Created by Profane Philosophies*

Dr. Hadi Sharifi: from *The Islamic as opposed to the modern philosophy of education.*

Dr. Hadi Sharifi is Professor of Philosophy and Sociology of Education in the University of Tehran, Iran. He identifies the true aims of education as being those to promote the awareness of God in the universe and draws pointed attention to the difference between Islamic and Western approaches to the question.

Usually in all modern philosophies a certain aspect of human nature – it might be the social, material, individual, biological or psychological aspect – is taken as the whole unique nature and being and accordingly an educational theory is developed, in which the unity and comprehensive character of human nature is as a result neglected. Thus, modern philosophies of education are first of all short-lived; secondly, every philosophical view of education, because of its very limited and contingent standpoint, can be easily criticized, negated and finally replaced by another; and thirdly, conflicts and never-ending struggles among different philosophical ideas and speculations seem to be a natural phenomenon. But from a traditional point of view this situation is critical, for the simple reason, that the sharp differences among the philosophical schools have brought confusion to the domain of educational theories, which usually try to define educational goals and orient the educational praxis.

The second problem is the problem of confusion among the educational aims and objectives in the modern world. This problem is apparently the result of a crisis in the value system, for if there is a relation between values and educational goals, then every goal, be it social, political or economic, implicitly or explicitly originates from a value perception. But the impact of this confusion on the domain of educational praxis is the lack of agreement and harmony, on the one hand among the educators and parents, and on the other, among psychologists, sociologists, economists and scientists, who are interested in the education of children and youth – but each from his own specialized and limited point of view. The critic of this chaotic situation in modern industrialized society has stimulated two different attitudes. One group of scholars has expressed doubt as to whether education necessarily must have aims. And the second group's attitude supports the postulate that the science of education, like every other science, must be neutral to values.

Another characteristic of the modern philosophies of education lies in their insistence upon the rationalistic aspect of the human being and thus their forgetfulness of the position and significance of the heart in education, an amnesis which does not affect the educational ideas and actions of a traditional culture. The problem of a pure rationalistic attitude in education lies in the fact that first of all the human being, in relation to his unity and comprehensive nature, is not purely a rationalistic creature, and much of his life – love, art and death – are not definable in a rationalistic way. Above all, there is the very wonderful fact of human life itself, which can only be 'explained' as a miracle. Secondly, in educating our children we have no right to concentrate our power and energy on one aspect of their existence and neglect the others. And finally, neglect of the position of the heart the very centre of the human being, that which can realize the Truth – in education, amounts to forgetfulness of the transcendental dimension of human life, to imprisonment in our limited sense perceptions and our worldly being forever, and to confinement to areas which are by no means appropriate to our Intellect and real Nature ('Fitrah').

Islamic education solves all problems by giving the spirit (heart) its supreme position in the system

To speak of the heart and its crucial importance in education as the only means of going beyond the ordinary level of consciousness and of realizing our real nature, is not understandable to the modern scientist and does not agree with the usual standards and norms of modern psychology only because modern science is limited to the empirical and the sensual.

For a modern scientist or psychologist, the heart is no more than a bodily organ, which has a certain biological function; thus it seems to us necessary to explain through the words of Gazzali, what traditional Muslims mean by the heart: 'When we speak of the heart, know that we mean the reality of man, which sometimes is called *ruh* (spirit) and sometimes *nafs* (soul); we do not mean that piece of flesh which lies in the left side of the chest; that organ is not worthy, for the cattle possess it, as do also the dead. It can be seen by ordinary eyes, and whatever can be seen by eyes belongs to this world, which is called the visible (*shahadah*) world. The reality of the heart is not of this world; it has come to this world as a stranger or a passer-by, and that visible piece of flesh is its vehicle and means, and all of the bodily features are its army, and it is the King of the whole body; the realization of God and the perception of His beauty is its function.'

Education is an integral part of life and so are philosophy and knowledge, and these are deeply interrelated. This close relation between philosophy, knowledge and education is a great significance in any traditional culture because the realization of the Ultimate Reality or the Absolute Truth occurs through the channel of spiritual training. The revelation or the existing spiritual doctrine usually provides a theoretical foundation, which describes the structure of Reality and the structure of human consciousness, the ontological status of the world and of all creatures, including human beings; and describes the way in which this reality is experienced by means of spiritual training. Because of this, there exists a sharp distinction between a traditional and a modern philosophy, and consequently between a traditional philosophy of education and a modern one. Because the realization of Truth by means of spiritual training is potentially open to every individual, the word of God pervades the whole culture, and so there remains no room for any kind of scepticism or agnosticism. And because of that Reality, unity and harmony appear in life. Values have a defined hierarchy, behaviour is structured, and stability appears on the scene of social life. This stability and also unity in a traditional culture are doubtless of a celestial nature; without the interference of God in our worldly life, unity (by which we do not mean uniformity) could never appear in social life, nor could this stability last for centuries, as is the case in Islamic civilization. If any further example is deemed necessary, one could compare the modern humanistic civilization of our age with the traditional civilization which existed before the Renaissance in Europe.

Modern man, who is interested in outer change of a social, political and economic nature, experiences the shape and structure of his settlement, town, country and world as always changing – this process is nowadays called development and progress. Changes in a traditional society however are directed towards the inner world of human beings, and nobody is exempted from this inner change except those who according to the Quran: 'have hearts, but understand not with them; they have eyes, but perceive not with them; they have ears, but they hear not with them. They are like cattle; nay, rather they are further astray. Those – they are the heedless.'

This inner change aims at the state of al-insān al-kamil, 'the perfect man' in Islamic education. Therefore this education is identified with a way which has a beginning but not an end, for the beginning of this way is the state of the human being as a terrestrial creature, hence limited and finite, but its end is the perfect man, who is Khalifat Allah (God's

49

earthly vice-gerent); this is the state of primordial man, and because this state is identified with the realization of the Unity of Being, and hence the Truth as Absolute, the end of this way is immersed in the Infinite.

Chapter Three

Diarchy in Education

Meaning

In nearly all Muslim countries there are two systems of education, the traditional and the modern.[1] Whereas in the early days of Islam there was only one system which taught purely theological subjects and mundane subjects like engineering and medicine, today the traditional system has the reading of the Quran (*Tajweed*, *Quiraat* and *Hifz*), Fiqh, Tafsir, Hadith and Arabic language and literature as core subjects. In some places classical logic (*Mantiq*) which ignores all developments in the West, mathematics and Islamic history are also taught. Islamic philosophy is included in a diluted form in one or two places.[2] Comparative religion, comparative study of Islamic and Western legal systems, social and natural sciences as they have developed in the West, are absent. Piety is the goal. The method does not include free inquiry or even free thinking. The teacher is regarded as the model for the taught. The challenges of modern civilization are not answered or even realized in their magnitude or depth. This system is also known in Morocco as the 'Fundamental System'.

Modern education means secular education according to which religious subjects are treated in the same way as non-religious subjects such as mathematics and geography. Nothing is taken for granted. The approach to knowledge is to some extent sceptical. The intention is to help the growth of a balanced personality whose intellect, emotions and physical self are balanced one against the other or, in other words, in harmony. There is an attempt to preserve a moral code but both teachers and the taught are finding it very difficult to subscribe to a common ethical norm. This system receives full government support because the governments realize that through this system they can produce trained people skilled enough to handle the problems of modern life or an industrialized society.

We described the presence of these two systems as diarchy in education because both systems claim the allegiance of a large number of men and women. In some cases, as in Turkey, Bangladesh and Indonesia, this allegiance has led to bloodshed and bitterness.[3]

The Historical Perspective

This word diarchy, therefore, needs to be understood in its historical context. It refers to the operation of two systems of education, one traditional and the other new, which are in many respects opposed to or at least inconsistent with each other and which for more than a century and a half Muslim educationists have been trying to reconcile. A few words on the historical background might be useful.

The Muslim world, by which, as stated in Chapter I, we mean countries inhabited primarily by Muslims or large Muslim majorities, was cut off from the mainstream of science and technology some time towards the end of the sixteenth century (some people will put the date even earlier)[4]. The result was that whereas Western Europe and later America went forward with new advances in knowledge these communities shut themselves off and were content to dwell in a kind of intellectual isolation. Then when the West encroached upon them suddenly, they woke up and found themselves unable to defend either their political or their intellectual independence. There followed an age of what is known as colonialism. For a time the Muslims stood aloof from what the new colonial masters tried to teach them. There was a widespread suspicion that the new education which the European powers sought to bring them was calculated to destroy their cultural heritage. But gradually they discovered that standing aloof from this education led to a progressive deterioration in their material conditions and further backwardness. So finally they revised their attitude and decided to have a closer look at what was being offered them.

The classic instance is the case of the large Muslim community in India.[5] As is well known, India was under Muslim rule for nearly seven centuries. When after the great battle of Plassey in 1757 the Muslims lost control in the eastern part of the sub-continent, the English took over and began reforming not only the system of administration but also the system of education. At first the idea was to leave the natives alone as far as possible and to train a handful of people who could aid them in running the country. Slowly it dawned on them that this would not do. The assumption of increasing administrative responsibility also

52

forced them to undertake new measures in areas other than administrative.

One of the first steps of this kind is represented by the establishment by Warren Hastings, the first Governor General of India, of a Madrasah in Calcutta which was designed to be a kind of sop to Muslim feeling. It was intended to provide facilities for Muslim children to study Arabic and Persian and such other subjects as traditional Muslim education considered legitimate. At the same time that this was being done the English rulers also set up new schools where children were invited to learn English. When the time came for the Government to choose recruits for various jobs, their choice fell naturally on those who knew English and the graduates of the Madrasah felt that they were being discriminated against. But then it was realized that the discrimination owed its justification to the fact that they did not know the new language, English, which the rulers needed for administrative purposes. The result was first serious protests and then some rethinking as to whether English really posed a threat to their culture and heritage. Finally, under pressure from the Muslims themselves, a new section was opened in the Madrasah called the Anglo-Persian Department. It provided some instruction in English along with the old courses. But this half-hearted measure did not go far enough to solve the problem that the Muslims were faced with. The situation was aggravated by the fact that the other Indian community, that is the Hindus, who had realized right from the beginning that the only way in which they could establish themselves materially was by mastering English and the new knowledge which it brought, had gone very far forward. All the statistics of the period show a wide disparity in employment between Muslims and Hindus. This continued until the great uprising of 1857 which made things much worse. There were reprisals against the Muslims and as a matter of policy they came to be left out of all important positions, so now they had a double handicap to contend with, their own backwardness in the matter of English plus the hostility of the rulers towards them on account of the part they played in the uprising of 1857.[6] It was felt by leading Muslim educationists that something on a planned scale needed to be done to change things.

Two men came forward at about the same time to suggest a reorientation. One was Nawab Abdul Lateef in Bengal and the other, Sir Syed Ahmad Khan in the north. They asked the community to end their boycott of English, reasoned that the English language could not seriously destroy their culture, and helped establish institutions which were designed to attract Muslim youth towards learning English and the new philosophy imported from the West. Sir Syed Ahmad, the better known of the two, lives in history as the founder of the Aligarh movement which later flowered into the famous Aligarh University which was until 1947 the principal seat of higher learning for Muslims in India.

What Sir Syed Ahmad and also his contemporary in Bengal tried to do was to provide a system which was in all respects modelled on the West but which gave facilities to the students to learn something about their history and religion along with what they learned from the West. There was actually no integration of the two kinds of education. Sir Syed's system proved a great success among those who wanted their children to have opportunities of employment in various areas of life but it was viewed with great suspicion by orthodox members of the Muslim community who felt that it did nothing to preserve the real Islamic heritage. They continued their boycott and went further by setting up new institutions designed to teach orthodox subjects along orthodox lines. The best known among them was the Madrasah at Deoband which to this day functions in what its detractors call a kind of backwater completely isolated from the rest of the world and keeping up the illusion that nothing outside its orbit has changed.

It is maintained by those who defend it that it has, like other Madrasahs, been performing a very useful role in preserving what would have been completely undermined, if not totally annihilated, by the impact of Western knowledge. The other important Islamic education centre where modern knowledge has not been neglected is the Nadwatul Ulema of Lucknow. The course introduced in Deoband known as Dars-i-Nizami has been modified by Nadwa.[7] Even then no reconciliation has as yet been possible.

Today all over the sub-continent, which means Bengal, i.e., Bangladesh, India and Pakistan, there are in existence orthodox institutions called Madrasahs along with modern schools and universities functioning as though in two geographically separated worlds with little or no intellectual contact between them, trying to serve two different kinds of need. There is widespread resentment over the fact that students from the Madrasahs do not receive what is considered to be their due share of economic privilege but their critics maintain that the kind of training which they have had renders them wholly unsuitable for the kind of work that the community needs. This dichotomy in education is tending all the time to weaken the community.

The critics say that it must be ended by an integrated system of education in which the distinction between the old learning and the new will be abolished and students will not have to have the feeling that there was a deep antagonism between the two. After all, they argue, until about the end of the sixteenth century no such division existed in the Muslim world. It is because the Muslims neglected the sciences and omitted to cultivate the knowledge which led to the discovery of new technology that all this trouble arose. Why then should it be impossible to restore the old unity?

We have already mentioned the experiment introduced by Sir Syed Ahmad. Towards the twenties of the present century, another experiment was undertaken by an educationist called Maulana Abu Nasr Waheed in Bengal. The system he introduced is known as the New Scheme. Unlike the Aligarh experiment it sought to integrate the old and the new according to a formula which obliged the students to study Arabic and religion as well as English and such modern subjects as algebra and geometry. These students took the same examinations as the others at modern schools and could afterwards join colleges and Universities. The idea was that they would be so well grounded in traditional learning that exposure to Western ideas at a later stage would not destroy their faith or undermine their belief in their own history and heritage. The New Scheme schools had their counterpart in a Department of Arabic Studies in the University of Dacca where also stress was laid on the combination of new and old learning. Nevertheless the real division between the old learning and the new has not disappeared. The majority of students in Universities in Bangladesh and their counterparts in Universities in Pakistan can obtain their degrees without any training in religion and history and they seem completely alienated from their heritage. With the passage of time this phenomenon has become increasingly pronounced. The scales are heavily weighted in favour of the new graduates. As the programmes of industrialization and modernization have gone forward, the tendency among the country's youth has been to treat the old learning as totally irrelevant to their needs. But sociologists feel alarmed at the results. The decay of faith, the undermining of the belief in old values is increasingly resulting in maladjustments and a widespread social malaise which must be counteracted if society is to preserve itself at all.

To give another example from an Arabic speaking area, consider the case of the great University of Al-Azhar in Cairo.[8] It has a history of over one thousand years. It claims to be one of the oldest existing universities in the world. There is no doubt that it played an extremely important role in the maintenance of Islam and in supplying Muslim administrations with the staff they needed in order to discharge their functions. But its syllabuses have not undergone any change for centuries with the result that when under the impact of its contact with the West Egypt woke up, it discovered that what Al-Azhar offered was very largely irrelevant to its contemporary needs. As in India, there was the same suspicion about Western learning, the same fear that it was inimical to Islam and would undermine the basic structure of Muslim society, but circumstances forced Egypt to set up new schools and universities. Nothing was done to reform Al-Azhar itself. It had to compromise eventually by allowing new wings to be added to it but its own structure remains exactly as it has been in the past. So here again we have the spectacle of two systems of education, one called modern and the other called orthodox, operating in the same country and between them there exists a feeling of rivalry which goes a long way towards weakening the foundations of Muslim society.

It is not that this phenomenon has not been encountered in other countries, say in countries like Japan and China. These two were for centuries isolated from the rest of the world and then had the painful realization that they had been left far behind by the West and a heavy price had to be paid by both. Japan has had the greater success in solving the problem. It had to pass through extremely painful experiences, short of a formal occupation by a foreign power, except after the Second World War which of course was due to different reasons. Its history during the nineteenth century provides a very interesting parallel to what happened in India and Egypt.

How to Reconcile the Two

The difference between the two systems that we have been talking about is not, however, just a difference of outward structure but a difference stemming from their approach to the aims of education. The old traditional system in Islam was anchored to a set of values derived from the Quran. It assumed that the true aim of education was the making of a man who was committed to God and who would learn to obey His commandments as laid down in the scripture. Such a person tried to understand all phenomena within and without in terms of the powers of God. On the other hand, the modern system, where it does not specifically exclude God, tries to do without Him in its explanation of the origins of the universe, or the phenomena with which man is in daily contact. The result on the one hand is a being deeply imbued with a sense of piety; on the other a being who thinks that there is no limit or end to the possibilities within him and that he can, without divine guidance, mould the world he lives in. There is from this point of view a basic similarity between the old European system which was based on Christian values and the Islamic system. Since the seventeenth century when the new philosophy began in the West, there has been an attempt to bypass, if not reject, God and this has been reflected in the kind of value system which has evolved. The Muslim, when exposed to Western thought, thus finds himself confronted with something which repudiates the basic premises on which the whole edifice of his religious and cultural life rests. This is the reason why the alliance from without between the modern Western system and the Islamic system does not seem to work. The Islamic system tries to impart a set of values which are contradicted by the modern system and people feel often bewildered and confused. But since the modern system is better geared to the kind of life that industrialization has created, the tendency on the part of a Muslim youth exposed to it without adequate precautions would be to assume that the old system which he has inherited from his own past is totally irrelevant to his modern needs. This is the problem that educationists are called upon to tackle.

It is clear that what we have called an outward alliance between the two systems such as was experimented with by Sir Syed Ahmad or Maulana Waheed will not do. What is needed is reform from within, by which we mean a complete revaluation of whatever learning a modern Muslim young man is called upon to acquire. There is at this point a problem which calls for some attention. It is clearly understood that there can be no question in the present age of rejecting modern science and technology. One cannot ask the community to go back to the days of isolation, nor will such a policy work if Muslims have to live in organized societies and free themselves from the oppressive burden of poverty and material backwardness. They must acquire the secrets which have led elsewhere to miraculous transformations. But what must be stressed is that they must not lose their own values in the process. Mere material progress cannot be an end in itself and the most advanced countries today are discovering to their cost that while they have succeeded in solving many of the material problems and been able to assure common man a standard of living of which his forefathers had no idea, he is far more unhappy and far more miserable than his predecessors were even a century ago. He is racked by a feeling of purposelessness; his society is plagued by an increasing growth of crime; there is no moral law which can hold it together. As long as a residue from the old Christian values lasted, he could complacently go along in the belief that the only things which mattered were material progress and economic advancement. Now that almost the last vestiges of Christianity have disappeared from the West there has appeared the terrible spectre of thoughtless crimes to which modern philosophy and modern science can find no answer. The innate respect for human life which all religions took for granted is itself at stake. The manner in which such issues as abortion, vivisection and genetic engineering are discussed shows an insensitivity to the very fundamentals of civilization. It sometimes seems that we are morally back in the Stone Age or even worse off. Marriage as an institution has almost broken down. Incest no longer arouses the moral repugnance it did. Homosexuality has been legalized. Even sexual assaults on children are sought to be excused. The reaction to all this manifests itself in a degree of lawlessness which has begun to worry the whole world. The Muslims believe that this pattern will be repeated in Muslim society if they do not take precautions in time against the inroads of Western ideas completely divorced from ethics and morality. We must return to where we started from, that is the discovery of an integrated system of education which will try to impart not only knowledge and information but also values. Diarchy must go but it cannot be abolished until the new learning from the West (which, as we have said, we cannot reject totally), has been subjected to careful scrutiny and review.

The correct mechanism of how to achieve a reconciliation of the old and the new has not so far been discovered. It is not a question of deciding in what exact proportions the two should be combined. This was what the reforms connected with the Aligarh movement in India or the New Scheme in Bengal tried to do. The point that needs to be borne in mind is that as long as we continue to speak in terms of proportions and ratios, we assume the existence of a line of demarcation between them. What is wanted is an integrated system in which the study of history or mathematics or nuclear physics would not be viewed as representing something utterly discordant with the study of the Quran, and so on.

Such an integration cannot arrive until Muslims themselves have so mastered the diverse fields of knowledge as to be able to produce books imbued with their own beliefs and ideals and assumptions. The present transition in which modern knowledge and religious education form an imperfect blend in our syllabuses has to be allowed to continue for some time. But its imperfections notwithstanding, this blend will have long-range effects in the right direction.

The immediate problem is whether the Western classification of knowledge is compatible with the Islamic concept of education. That the Western classification should reflect the Western approach to education is not a matter that should perturb us. The question is whether in advance of the arrival of books by Muslims, written in accordance with the Muslim outlook, we can afford to alter the existing classification without creating serious impediments to the progress of Muslim societies. Considering our present dependence on Western books, in higher education in particular, a policy of gradualness would seem to be the answer. So the transition in the matter of text-books must also mean a transition in respect of the organization of knowledge in our educational institutions. To try to reclassify knowledge in the absence of the right kind of books would be putting the cart before the horse. However distasteful the present classification may appear, pragmatism suggests that we should bear with it for a transitional period and not attempt an immediate change.

There is, however, one aspect of the matter on which work must go ahead which is what the new Islamic classification ought to be. Has there been any advance in knowledge requiring the classification associated with Islam to be re-examined? This conceptual scrutiny need not be put off, indeed it must not be put off until the arrival of the new books. For the writing of these books will depend upon the priorities in education being fixed by our scholars at the conceptual level. That is the task facing us in the immediate future.

The scholars from whom we have reproduced some extracts are more or less agreed on this. They differ in the degree of their emphasis but they are unanimous that these contradictory systems cannot be allowed to continue for ever. Some may be a little more partial to modern Western education than others but basically there is no difference in their ideas and what they say about the need for an integrated system is supported also by scholars elsewhere. They have all tried to isolate what is basic and fundamental in Muslim education and what outward trappings from the Western system can easily be dispensed with. They maintain also that as long as Muslim society continues to rely upon text-books borrowed from the West, the problem will stay with us, because text-books, whether they are text-books on physics or chemistry or political science, are imbued with the ethical values of the writers and the only way in which this problem can be tackled is by Muslim writers coming forward to produce their own text-books which will be free from the kind of bias which informs Western writings. Of course it is to be understood that this process cannot be carried too far, at least not at present. If Muslims waited for the whole body of text-books to be revised they would probably have to call a halt to whatever progress in modern education they have made. The only sensible remedy is to formulate a programme which will cail for a review of text-books and at the same time so educate children at the lower stages that they will develop within themselves a critical apparatus capable of beating back the attacks of alien philosophy and thought. It is along these lines that a new programme needs to be drawn up.

Extracts

1. Unity in Early Islamic System of Education

(i) *Unity provided by the teaching of the Quran and the Hadith and the Islamic attitude to knowledge*
Dr. S. M. Hossain: from *A Plea for Modern Islamic University in Muslim Countries*

Dr. S. M. Hossain was Professor and Head of the Department of Arabic and Islamic Studies at the University of Dacca and then Vice-Chancellor of the same University. He is at present Professor Emeritus of Arabic at Decca University. He discusses the Muslim attitude to knowledge in the past and shows how Muslim thinkers classified knowledge in the light of the Quran. The central symbol of the Islamic revelation is a book and learning is thus inseparable from religion. The mosque was the first place where teaching was carried on and it is still carried on there. Quranic verses and prophetic sayings emphasize the importance of learning.

The Quran is the first Book in which mankind was exhorted to attain perfection by acquiring knowledge through reading and writing. The frequent mention of writing, reading and the pen in the Quran and particularly in the very first revelation of the Prophets (S), is rather amazing since it is a well-known fact that not only was the use of writing a rare novelty in the then Arabia, but the Prophet (S) was himself unacquainted with writing and reading. The revelation was being granted to the Prophet (S) to bring him and through him the whole of humanity to perfection. Imbued with this spirit, Muslim scholars applied themselves to develop an elaborate system of education which produced men capable of undertaking the responsibilities of this world and the world hereafter. They developed this system as a result of the teaching of the Quran – the mission of Prophet Muhammad, peace and blessings of Allah be on him. . . The study of the Quran and Hadith, the twin fountainhead of knowledge, created all the impulse and impetus for the cultivation and advancement of Islamic learning.

(ii) *Arts and Sciences of the Islamic World*

Dr. Seyyed Hossein Nasr's summary of *Ibn Khaldun's classification* from *The Muqaddimah: An Introduction to History*, translated from the Arabic by Franz Rosenthal, New York, 1958: from *Science and Civilization in Islam*, New York 1970, pp. 63–64

In his Introduction to History, Ibn Khaldun surveys the arts and sciences of the Islamic world, defining the aim and scope of each discipline. Although his Introduction was not itself universally read during the later periods, his classification contains in summary fashion the plan according to which the arts and sciences have, in fact, been studied in most religious Islamic schools during the past several centuries. Even if many of these schools, especially in the Sunni world, have not studied all the subjects enumerated by Ibn Khaldun, they have usually accepted the principles of his classification, which can be considered the final version of the Islamic division of the sciences.

Ibn Khaldun's division may be summarized as follows:

A. Sciences studied in the Islamic World:
   – philosophical and intellectual (such as can be learned by man naturally through the use of his innate reason and intelligence);
   – transmitted (such as can be learned only by transmission, going back ultimately to the founder of the science and in the case of religious sciences to the origin of the Revelation)

B. Philosophical or Intellectual Sciences:
   1. Logic
   2. Natural Sciences or Physics; Medicine; Agriculture
   3. Sciences of being beyond Nature, or Metaphysics; Magic and Talisman; Science of the occult properties of letters of the Alphabet; Alchemy
   4. Sciences dealing with Quantity:
      Geometry (plain and spherical optics); Arithmetic (property of numbers, are of calculation, algebra, commercial transactions, calculation of inheritance); Music; Astronomy (the making of astronomical tables, motion of heavenly bodies, Astrology).

C. Transmitted Sciences:
   1. Quran, its interpretation and recitation
   2. Hadith, the sayings of the Prophets and their chain of transmission
   3. Jurisprudence, sacred law
   4. Theology
   5. Sufism (*al-tasawwuf*)
   6. Linguistic sciences, such as grammar, lexicography, and literature

Not all of the sciences enumerated above have always been taught in all of the institutions of learning which have constituted the most formal and official educational organizations in the Islamic world. But they have been transmitted from one generation to another through either formal instruction or private teaching, and they must therefore be regarded as a part of the intellectual life of Islam.

(iii) *Unity provided by the ideal order behind the curriculum*
Al-Farabi (c. 870–950): as commented upon, quoted and translated by Dr. Seyyed Hossain Nasr, Professor of Philosophy of Tehran University and at one time Chancellor of Aryamehr University, Iran, in his book *Science and Civilization in Islam*, New York, Mentor books, 1970, pp. 71–79

Although the curriculum of the madrasah has not been the same during all periods of Islamic history, and in all parts of the Islamic world, there has been a general ideal order, which has always remained in the background, and has often been followed, especially in the schools where the philosophic or *awā'il* sciences have been taught. Early in Islamic history, the famous philosopher al-Fārābī, whose classification of the sciences we have just discussed, had already turned to a consideration of the order in which the study of the sciences should be undertaken, and the disciplines that should be mastered. In his *Attainment of Happiness* he writes:

> The first genus of beings into which one should inquire is that which is easier for man and in which perplexity and mental confusion are less likely to occur. This is the genus of numbers and magnitudes. . . .
> It is characteristic of this science that inquires into numbers and magnitudes that the principles of instruction in it are identical with the principles of being. Hence all demonstrations proceeding from its principles combine the two things – I mean they give an account of the thing's existence and of why it exists: all of them are demon-

strations of both *that* the thing is and *why* it is. Of the principles of being, it employs [only the formal, that is] *what* the thing is and *by what* and *how* it is, to the exclusion of the other three. For numbers and magnitudes, in the mind and stripped from the material, have no principles related to their genus apart from the principles of their being just mentioned. They possess the other principles only on account of their coming into being by nature or the will, that is, when they are assumed to be in materials. Since this science does not inquire into them as being in materials, it does not deal with what is extraneous to them so far as they are not in materials.

One begins, then, first with numbers [that is, arithmetic], proceeds next to magnitudes [that is, geometry], and then to all things in which number and magnitude are inherent essentially (such as optics, and the magnitudes in motion, which are the heavenly bodies), music, the study of weights, and mechanics. In this way one begins with things that may be comprehended and conceived irrespective of any material. He then proceeds to things that can be comprehended, conceived, and intellected by only slight reference to a material; next, the things that can only be comprehended, conceived, and intellected with slightly more reference to a material. He continues thus toward the things wherein number and magnitude inhere, yet that which can be intellected in them does not become intelligible except by progressively greater reference to the material. This will lead him to the heavenly bodies, then music, then the study of weights and mechanics, where he is forced to deal with things that become intelligible only with difficulty, or that cannot exist, except when they are in materials. One is now forced to include principles other than *what*, *by what* and *how*. He has come to the borderline between the genus that does not have any other principle of being apart from *what* it is, and the genus whose species possess the four principles. It is at this point that the natural principles come into view.

At this juncture one ought to set out to know the beings that possess the four principles of being: that is, the genus comprising the things that can be perceived by the intellect only when they are in materials. (Indeed the materials are called [by some] *the* natural things.) The inquirer ought to seize upon all the principles of instruction – that is, the first premises – relative to the genus consisting of *particular* things. He should also look into the primary knowledge he has and adopt from it whatever he recognizes as appropriate for being made into principles of instruction in this science.

63

He then should begin to inquire into bodies and into things that are in bodies. The genera of bodies constitute the world and the things comprised by the world. In general, they are the genera of sensible bodies or of such bodies that possess sensible qualities: that is, the heavenly bodies; then earth, water, air and things of this kind (fire, vapour, etc.); then the stony and mineral bodies on the surface of the earth and inside it; and finally, plants, irrational animals, and rational animals. He should give an account of (a) the fact of the being, and (b) all the principles of being of every one of these genera, and of every one of the species of every genus: that is, in every problem relative to them, he should give an account of (a) the fact *that* the thing is, and (b) *what, by what*, and *how* it is, *from what* it is, and *for what* it is. In none of them is he to confine himself to its proximate principles. Instead he should give an account of the principles of its principles and of the principles of the principles of its principles, until he arrives at its ultimate corporeal principle.

The principles of instruction in most of what this science comprises are distinct from the principles of being, and it is through the principles of instruction that one comes to know the principles of being. For in every genus of natural things the principles of instruction are inferior to the principles of being, since the principles of being in such a genus are the grounds to which the principles of instruction owe their existence. Hence the ascent toward knowledge of the principles of being of every genus or species can be made only through things that originate in these principles. If these happen to be proximate principles A that in turn have other principles B, the proximate principles A should be employed as principles of instruction from which to ascend to knowledge of their principles B. Then, when these principles B become known, one proceeds from them to the principles of these principles, C, until he arrives at the ultimate principles of being in the genus. If, after ascending from the principles of instruction to the principles of being and the knowledge of the principles of being, there are (in addition to the primary cognitions from which we ascended to the principles) other things originating from these principles, and which are still unknown, then we proceed to use these principles of being as principles of instruction and so come to know the other, inferior things. In relation to the other things, our principles are now both principles of instruction and principles of being. We follow this procedure in every genus of sensible bodies and in each of the species of every genus.

When one finally comes to inquire into the heavenly bodies and investigate the principles of their being, this inquiry into the principles of their being, will force one to look for principles that are not natures or natural things, but beings more perfect than nature and natural things. They are also not bodies or in bodies. Therefore one needs another kind of investigation here and another science that inquires exclusively into beings that are metaphysical. At this point one is again standing between two sciences: the science of nature and [metaphysics or] the science of what is *beyond* natural things in the order of investigation and instruction and *above* them in the order of being.

When the inquirer finally reaches the stage of investigating the principles of the being of animals, he will be forced to inquire into the soul and learn about psychical [or animate] principles, and from there ascend to the inquiry into the rational animal. As he investigates the principles of the latter, he will be forced to inquire into (1) *what, by what,* and *how,* (2–3) *from what,* and (4) *for what* it is. It is here that he acquaints himself with the intellect and things intelligible. He needs to investigate (1) *what* the intellect is and *by what* and *how* it is, and (2–3) *from what* and (4) *for what* it is. This investigation will force him to look for other principles that are not bodies or in bodies, and that never were or ever will be in bodies. This inquiry into the rational animal will thus lead him to the same conclusion as the inquiry into the heavenly bodies. Now he acquaints himself with incorporeal principles that are to the beings below the heavenly bodies as those incorporeal principles (with which he became acquainted when investigating the heavenly bodies) are to the heavenly bodies. He will acquaint himself with principles for the sake of which the soul and the intellect are made, and with the ends and ultimate perfection for the sake of which man is made. He will know that the natural principles in man and in the world are not sufficient for man's coming to that perfection for the sake of whose achievement he is made. It will become evident that man needs some rational, intellectual principles with which to work toward that perfection.

At this point the inquirer will have sighted another genus of things, different from the metaphysical. It is incumbent on man to investigate what is included in this genus: that is, the things that realize for man his objective through the intellectual principles that are in him, and by which he achieves that perfection that became known in natural science. It will become evident concomitantly that these rational principles are not mere *causes* by which man attains the perfection for which he is made. Moreover, he will know that these rational principles also supply many things to natural being other than those supplied by nature. Indeed man arrives at the ultimate perfection (whereby he attains that which renders him truly substantial) only when he labours with these principles toward achieving this perfection. Moreover, he cannot labour toward this perfection except by exploiting a large number of natural beings and until he manipulates them to render them useful to him for arriving at the ultimate perfection he should achieve. Furthermore, it will become evident to him in this science that each man achieves only a portion of that perfection, and what he achieves of this portion varies in its extent, for an isolated individual cannot achieve all the perfections by himself and without the aid of many other individuals. It is the innate disposition of every man to join another human being or other men in the labour he ought to perform: this is the condition of every single man. Therefore, to achieve what he can of that perfection, every man needs to stay in the neighbourhood of others and associate with them. It is also the innate nature of this animal to seek shelter and to dwell in the neighbourhood of those who belong to the same species, which is why he is called the *social* and *political* animal. There emerges now another science and another inquiry that investigates these intellectual principles and the acts and states of character with which man labours toward this perfection. From this, in turn, emerge the science of man and political science.

He should begin to inquire into the metaphysical beings and, in treating them, use the methods he used in treating natural things. He should use as their principles of instruction the first premises that happen to be available and are appropriate to this genus, and in addition, the demonstrations of natural science that fit as principles of instruction in this genus. These should be arranged according to the order mentioned above, until one covers every being in this genus. It will become evident to whomever investigates these things that none of them can possess any material at all; one ought to investigate every one of them only as to (1) *what* and *how* it is, (2–3) *from what* agent and (4) *for what* it is. He should continue this investigation until he finally reaches a being that cannot possess any of these principles at all (either *what* it is or *from what* it is or *for what* it is) but is itself the first principle of all the aforementioned beings: it is itself that *by* which, *from* which, and *for* which they are, in the most perfect modes in which a thing can be a principle for the beings, modes free from all defects. Having understood this, he should investigate next what properties the other beings possess as a consequence of their having *this* being as their principle and the cause of their being. He should begin with the being whose rank is higher than the rest (that is, the one nearest to the first principle), until he terminates in the being whose rank is inferior to the rest (that is, the one furthest from the first principle). He will thus come to know the ultimate causes of the beings. This is the divine inquiry into them. For the first principle is the divinity, and the principles that come after it – and are not bodies or in bodies – are the divine principles.

Then he should set out next upon the science of man and investigate the *what* and the *how* of the purpose for which man is made, that is, the perfection that man must achieve. Then he should investigate all the things by which man achieves this perfection or that are useful to him in achieving it. These are the good, virtuous, and noble things. He should distinguish them from things that obstruct his achieving this perfection. These are the evils, the vices, and the base things. He should make known *what* and *how* every one of them is, and *from what* and *for what* it is, until all of them become known, intelligible and distinguished from each other. This is political science. It consists of knowing the things by which the citizens of cities attain happiness through political association in the measure that innate disposition equips each of them for it. It will become evident to him that political association and the totality that results from the association of citizens in cities correspond to the association of the bodies that constitute the totality of the world. He will come to see in what are included in the totality constituted by the city and the nation the likenesses of which are included in the total world. Just as in the world there is a first principle, then other principles subordinate to it, beings that proceed from these principles, other beings subordinate to these beings, until they terminate in the beings with the lowest rank in the order of being, the nation or the city includes a supreme commander, followed by other commanders, followed by other citizens, who in turn are followed by other citizens, until they terminate in the citizens with the lowest rank as citizens and as human beings. Thus the city includes the likenesses of the things included in the total world.

This, then, is theoretical perfection. As you see, it comprises knowledge of the four kinds of things by which the citizens of cities and nations attain supreme happiness. What still remains is that these four should be realized and have actual existence in nations and cities while conforming to the account of them given by the theoretical sciences.

2. Refutation of Duality

(i) *A brief historical account of duality in the Arab world and its bad effects.* Professor Ahmed al-Beely: from *The Islamic Concept of Educational Curricula.*

Professor Ahmed al-Beely, Professor in the Faculty of Shariah, The University of Riyadh, discusses the bad effects of this duality on every aspect of Muslim society.

There was one general curriculum in all Muslim countries even after the invasions of the Mongols, the Tartars, and the Crusaders. The establishment of religious institutes and secular schools side by side in Arab and Muslim countries started only after foreign occupation in the 19th and 20th centuries. Occupation powers decided to wage war against the main cultural elements of the colonized people, but in a cunning and deceitful fashion, they planned to leave religious teaching institutes to die out gradually for nobody would enrol in them for fear of getting no jobs after graduation or of getting a low salary even if jobs were available. Consequently they left Al-Azhar, Al-Zaitonna, Al-Maahad Al-Elmy of Sudan, and similar institutes to carry on with their religious education, and founded the so-called secular schools of four stages. They gave those new schools beautifully and purposely designed buildings, provided them with equipment and apparatus, and trained teachers in various subjects. Government offices were eager to employ the new graduates in various jobs. Parents saw that secular education yielded its fruit in the form of respectable jobs with big salaries and so they rushed to enrol their children in those schools, while the religious institutes were left for either some of the children whose families were concerned with religion, or the children of poor families. The graduates of those institutes had no prospect of employment except as teachers of language and religion, mosque *imams*, preachers or, in a very few cases, Muslim Court Judges in some countries.

When both religious and secular types of education produced graduates in the Arab countries, the products of secular education held top positions in the armed forces, police, civil service and public administration, while the products of religious education were employed only as judges in Muslim courts, mosque *imams*, preachers or teachers of language and religion. A cultural and class struggle broke out between these two groups, and each group accused the other of being less educated than itself. The secular graduates boasted of knowing a foreign language and familiarity with experimental sciences, general history of mankind, geography, mathematics, etc. The religious graduates boasted of their excellent achievement in memorizing and reciting the Quran, familiarity with jurisprudence, theology and other branches of Islamic studies, and familiarity with linguistic sciences such as morphology, grammar, rhetoric, prosody etc.

Measures taken by the occupation powers made people firmly convinced that it was only the Sheikhs ('ulama) who should be concerned with the study of religion and adherence to it, and that secular schools produced another type of educated people who should not, and were not, expected to understand religion or adhere to it. Consequently people in most Arab Muslim countries, which suffered from that sort of dichotomy, would forgive an Effendi who did something wrong, but would not forgive a Sheikh for doing the same thing, because in their view the Sheikh was closely connected with religion but not the Effendi. The dichotomy that was created by occupation authorities is similar to the dichotomy established in Western countries where religion is completely divorced from everyday life, associated only with churches on Sundays and with priests, monks and nuns, to the exclusion of other men and women. This dichotomy is alien to Islam, because there is no clergy in Islam; there are only specialized scholars in religion as opposed to laymen who do not specialize in studying religion.

The effect of duality on Legislation and jurisdiction

Graduates of law schools and faculties continued what the foreign rulers started in the field of legislation. They enacted laws which were not derived from Islamic Jurisprudence, but from the laws of the occupying country, be it England, France or any other. Considering their educational background, those graduates could not possibly consult the original sources of Islamic jurisprudence (Shari'ah), because they did not study them or develop the ability to deduce laws from them and understand their terms. Even those who were familiar with Islamic jurisprudence through personal effort, were not allowed by the government to introduce Islamic laws; and moreover, if they suggested those laws and published them in books, the government would not enforce them.

It is not surprising then that the brainwashed Muslims continued what the colonialists started in an attempt to sever all connection between Islam and the current life of the muslims. It was this imminent danger that induced the authorities in the land of the two Holy Mosques (*Al-Haramain*) to present the problem to a number of those concerned with Islamic thought, and invite them to investigate its different aspects and suggest a radical solution which could be implemented by all Muslim countries. Some of the countries which used two different types of curricula from the beginning of the primary stage attempted to solve the problem by adding all the curricula of secular schools, in spite of their drawbacks and enormous content, to the curricula used in religious institutes. But that was not an effective remedy, because it added to the burden of the institutes' students, and consequently they could achieve neither an adequate command of their main subjects, nor the same standard in secular subjects as their counterparts in schools. In point of fact a large number of the institutes' students made greater efforts at mastering the modern subjects (such as physical science, mathematics and geography, as distinguished from religious and Arabic studies) and neglected their main subjects, only because modern subjects led to science faculties and eventually meant respectable jobs, with big salaries and prestige attached to them. Religious institutes therefore lost some of the bright students because nothing attracted them to stay and graduate from them.

Some other countries kept both types of curriculum as they were, because they believed that that was the best policy, but they tried to attract students to religious education by prizes, scholarships, and other rewards.

Yet other countries completely abolished religious education institutes, and decided that students selected to pursue Arabic and Islamic studies at universities should be able to score high marks in Arabic and religious education in their pre-university examination. These countries kept primary, intermediate, and secondary school curricula as they were; the number of religious subjects was not increased, and no rewards were provided for students who achieved an exceptionally high standard in Arabic and religious education. Consequently bright students made greater efforts to study the subjects that enabled them to join such faculties as those of law, engineering, medicine, science and agriculture, and hardly any student paid special attention to Arabic and Islamic subjects. Islamic universities had to follow the policy of 'something is better than nothing', and required that every applicant for a place should have passed the Secondary Education Certificate Examination and obtained high marks in Arabic and religious education.

This solution, in my view, does not help Islamic universities to recruit students of the same intelligence and learning capacity as those who join the faculties of medicine and engineering, for example. There is an urgent need to draw an educational plan which is free from all the faults pointed out in the religious curricula and institutes, and in the secular curricula and schools. The new plan should discuss the curricula, text-books, teacher training, school life and harmony between school life and life outside schools. That kind of harmony cannot be achieved without cooperation between the mass media and the ministries of education. For we can never establish the desired Muslim society by reforming schools, curricula and teachers, while the press, radio, television and the cinema are left without control, and are pouring out material which does not abide by the principles or the teachings of Islam.

(ii) *Integration through common courses and specialization in different branches*

Professor Ahmed al-Beely discusses the claims made by the supporters of duality and suggests various courses including a general principle for writing text-books.

A Muslim country is in great need of such knowledge as can raise its material standards. One group of its students need to specialize in different secular subjects, but another group should specialize in religious subjects. The former may study such religious subjects as give them sufficient knowledge of the beliefs and observances in Islam, and moral principles that improve their character. They may also study enough Arabic to enable them to read it with understanding, write and speak it comprehensibly and correctly, and translate into it efficiently from other living languages.

This group specializing in religious subjects may study a small number of secular subjects, but must devote the greater part of their life-time to the preservation of both Islamic and Arabic legacies and must safeguard them against any break in the continuity of the linguistic tradition, or the failure to transmit the cultural heritage to posterity; and against misconceptions of religious beliefs, observances, and laws of transactions. Some of the members of this group should reach the stage of specialization where they can give independent opinions in the

71

absence of a text (*ijtihād*), and can discriminate between the authentic and the spurious, the true and the false, because of their long experience in linguistic and religious research.

This group will never reach the high standard required unless they memorize the Quran together with the Prophet's Tradition and the sayings of their venerable forefathers. They should also add to their repertoire a great deal of the literary works, prose and poetry, produced by Arab writers during the period of pristine purity in the history of Arabic writings. The memorization of such works will improve their sense of judgement, and make them efficient guides and reliable authorities for others on matters of religion, language, and life in accordance with Islamic principles. This is the Islamic and Arabic legacy, these are its origins and sources and special institutions should be established for their study. Students should join these in their childhood and engage in memorizing the Holy Quran and reciting it; studying exegesis and principles of deductions followed by previous religious leaders; and memorizing a large number of the Prophet's Traditions. It is difficult to provide such specialized training as is required in religious and linguistic studies at the university stage alone, as the advocates of unification at the primary and intermediate stages claim.

However, it is essential that those specializing in Islamic and Arabic studies should take, during the three pre-university stages, adequate courses in mathematics, physical science, geography and the general history of mankind; and should be given the opportunity to learn one foreign language to the level of reading with comprehension. The knowledge of a foreign language is necessary for a preacher of Islam, for it enables him to read what was and is written about Islam in that other language, to defend Islam against its detractors and to enrich Arabic by translating good literature into it. He can also preach Islam in a foreign language to its speakers. . . .

A Final Word

The text-book is the most important educational tool, since it is the student's companion at home and at school. The spirit of Islam should, therefore, be the dominant feature in all text-books on whatever subject. Moreover, all our courses, books and teaching materials should have as their central theme the relationship between God, Man and the Universe. It should be stressed that God always gives and man receives, God is worshipped and man is the worshipper. The universe is intended by God for the service of man so that man can worship God. Man needs help and God created the universe to help man. There are

1. theological studies about God,
2. humanities about man, and
3. natural studies about the universe.

Text-book writers, teachers, and learners should always remember these relationships between God, Man and the Universe, and should always draw attention to them and stress them, so that Muslims may always worship God, believe in Him alone, and refer to his Shari'ah only for decisions on every new issue in their lives.

When this is done, the Muslim world will not be the same as it is nowadays. Muslims will then discover their latent powers, release them, become worthy of shouldering the responsibility that was left for them to bear, and rise to fulfil their mission, which is the propagation of Islam in the whole world. 'My success (in my task) can only come from God, in Him I trust, and unto Him I look.' And my last words are: 'Praise be to God, the Cherisher and Sustainer of the Worlds.'

Chapter Four

Conceptual Crisis in Social and Natural Sciences

Traditional vis-à-vis Modern Concepts

Education is a process that helps the balanced growth of the total personality of man. This growth is possible only when society believes in a common concept of man. Man, according to Islam, is composed of spirit, soul and body. 'He is at once a spirit and matter. He is a unity as an individual and his individuality is referred to as the self; He is endowed with attributes bestowed by Allah.'[1] From this point of view the training imparted to a Muslim must be such that faith is infused into the whole of his personality, creating in him an emotional attachment to Islam which enables him to follow the Quran and the Sunnah and be governed by the Islamic system of values. This training is possible only when education is so planned that the different branches of knowledge are considered as an integrated unit and not as completely independent items having completely different conceptual origins.

During the early days of Islam, knowledge was generally classified into two categories:[2] 1. Basic fundamental knowledge derived directly from the Quran and the Sunnah; and 2. Knowledge acquired by man primarily with the help of his intellect and experiments. But these two were always integrated through a system of concepts which have been variously described by different philosophers and thinkers of the Muslim world such as Al-Farabi, Avicenna and al-Ghazzali. This classification was later on reordered by Ibn Khaldun in his *Introduction to History*.[3] He divided knowledge into عَقْلِي and نَقْلِي which means 'philosophical and intellectual (such as can be learned by man naturally through the use of his innate reason and intelligence)' and 'transmitted (such as can be learned only by transmission, going back ultimately to the founder of the sciences and in the case of religious sciences to the origin of the Revelation)'.[4] This division, however, did not split knowledge into completely separate compartments as both of these were found essentially integrated through the central symbol of

74

the Islamic revelation, that is the Holy Book. For that reason learning was made inseparable from religion.

While speaking of this unity Hossein Nasr indicates that 'although the curriculum of the madrassas has not been the same through all periods of Islamic history and in all parts of the Islamic world, there has been a general ideal order, which has always remained in the background, and has often been followed, especially in the schools where the philosophic *awā'il* sciences have been taught'.[5] He then goes on to quote Al-Farabi on this basis of the classification of knowledge and the ideal order which integrates different branches.[6]

In the West also there was an integration which we notice in the classification of knowledge by Saint Thomas Aquinas.[7] But gradually the division of divine and secular branches of knowledge became more and more pronounced and the two branches got separated during the fifteenth and sixteenth centuries.[8] By the time we reach the end of the seventeenth century the secular branches of knowledge were practically segregated from the divine and the source of the secular branches was considered to be the human intellect which need not have any relation with divine inspiration.[9] This secularization led to the emergence of those branches of knowledge which were categorized in 1957 by the Presidents of American Universities in the Harvard Report as 'Humanities, Social Sciences and Natural Sciences'. It is this classification which has become popular not merely in America and Europe but also in the Muslim world. In planning the curriculum of American universities Divinity was excluded from compulsory teaching and students were expected to have a basic knowledge of all these three branches whereas in most countries in the Muslim world religious instruction was included. When we go through the different concepts of acquiring these three branches of knowledge we notice a complete separation between the spiritual and the intellectual and material aspects of human personality. In other words, it is not one but many contradictory concepts of human personality which are governing the education system in the West. It is here that we find the conceptual crisis in Humanities, Social and Natural Sciences.

The crisis in the Muslim world lies in the prevalence of two contradictory notions, the one that is derived from religion and had been the basis of the Islamic system of education in the past, and the other that is at the root of the secularized system that the Muslim world has imported from the West. This conflict is also strongly resented by the religious thinkers of the West but they themselves have been unable to stop the onrush of secularism and the influence of the secular concept of human personality. The problem is more acute in the sphere of Social and Natural Sciences than in the sphere of Humanities though in so far as the separation of these branches from religion is concerned, there is a common approach to all the three branches in the modern system of education. Religious knowledge is considered as a class apart and an arena to be looked after mainly by religious people, therefore by people who believe in divine inspiration. Unfortunately, even in the religious sphere, we find in Western schools a new tendency to regard religion just as a common human fabrication to be treated as a kind of information to be imparted to children by anybody who has some external knowledge about this subject and who may or may not be a believer. So far as the other branches of knowledge are concerned, various notions about human personality have created complications. As a result the easiest way out has been to evolve a so-called scientific method which is regarded as objective and whose methodology leads to observation, data collection and generalization. In view of the fact that something beyond this observable reality is expected to penetrate into literature and the fine arts, it is separated from Social and Natural Sciences and treated in the Humanities as something subjective and consequently less reliable from the point of view of truth-realization.

Modern Methodology in Social Sciences and its Shortcomings

There are serious shortcomings in this methodology if we look at it from the Islamic point of view. These shortcomings have been analyzed by various Muslim thinkers, Hossein Nasr in *Islam and the Plight of Modern Man* and other scholars who attended the First Conference on Muslim Education held at Mecca in 1977, such as Ismail Faruqi in his essay on 'Islamising the Social Sciences', Professor Elkholy in his article 'Towards an Islamic Anthropology', Dr. Mohammad Nejatullah Siddiqi in his essay on 'The Teaching of Economics', Professor Abdul Hamid Siddiqi in his essay on 'The Islamic Concept of History', Professor Abdul Hamid el-Hashimi in his essay 'The Islamic Concept of Psychology' and Dr. Waqar Ahmed Husaini in his essay 'Humanistic Social Sciences Studies in Higher Technical Education'.

The common principle that has so far emerged out of these cogitations is based on the difference between the Islamic concept of human personality and the concept or concepts governing these branches of knowledge. It is obvious that no solution is possible through any reconciliation because it is not possible to reconcile two completely different concepts of man. In the case of Islam, one has to accept if one believes in religion that man has a spirit and that spiritual and moral aspects of his personality cannot be separated from any form of human activity whether individual or social. Therefore, human behaviour cannot be isolated and separated from its moral and spiritual components. The methodology of Social Sciences as it has been developed in the West has no means of dealing with the spiritual. As the Western secular thinkers leave out the spiritual element in man and try to be 'objective', they ignore value perception and hence they make morality a social phenomenon. In Islam man is a spiritual being; he has a definite role to play in this world and his activities are governed by certain basic principles of conduct which if he violates, he will degenerate, but when he observes those rules of conduct he becomes a 'good' man. It is this concept of the good that permeates all religious thinking and it is on the basis of this concept that social laws are formulated. Therefore, when one is studying the human psyche as an individual entity or carrying on investigations into human behaviour in society, one is compelled to go beyond observable data into a reality which deals with attitudes, values and judgements.

The Individual

In the case of the individual, there is a long standing tradition of the Islamic concept of mind which is completely ignored in modern psychology. Whereas in the past the Islamic concept of psychology used to be taught in Muslim universities, it is now neglected and ignored in modern universities in the Muslim world. The limitations of modern psychology have not been thoroughly analyzed. Both Western and Eastern psychological studies nowadays confine their fields of interest to single aspects of man such as physical drives, or the sexual instinct, or the aberrant behaviour or correlative or reflexive instincts and thus fail to give an integrated picture of a human being. As Dr. Hashimi has pointed out, because of this limitation modern psychological studies are scientifically deficient. He also points out that these studies have serious shortcomings from the practical point of view because the moral factor is banished from the practical sphere.

Man's mind is a by-product of three different forces, spirit (*ruh*), the

77

intellect (*'aql*) and the passionate soul attached to the body (*nafs*).[10] The spirit is considered to be directly related to the being of God and is thus a source of Man's consciousness of existence beyond this material existence. The intellect is the universal principle of all intelligence and is the source of Man's logical thinking and concept formulation and the soul or nafs or self has stages and levels of perfection. When it is separated from the spirit and is controlled by external and physical desires and passions, it is known as the lowest self. The second stage is that in which the mind hovers between spiritual domination and domination by passion and worldly demands. At the last stage, the intellect accepts the mastery of the spirit and responds to spiritual domination and keeps material demands under legitimate control. Different schools of human psychology emerged among Muslim thinkers in the past but those have been ignored by modern thinkers in the West and also in the East. Only in the traditional Islamic system of education that branch of human knowledge is studied. It is, therefore, necessary to accept the tools invented by modern psychologists but apply them within the framework of Islamic principles. This is not possible so long as we do not accept the Islamic concept of man. If we start with no accepted concept of man, experiments which are purely external can never lead us to an integrated concept given by God. We shall continuously be biased by our partial realizations of truth and we shall never be able to have a comprehensive view of man's personality. It is only after we accept the given concept of mind and proceed from this assumption and start experimenting by keeping those norms in mind, that we shall be able to give a more comprehensive analysis of the human psyche – an analysis which will also enter into the sphere of values and morals provided these values are spiritual and in accordance with man's innate nature.

Society: Unity versus Multiplicity

When we analyze man in society or man's social behaviour in the context of the world in which he lives it is necessary for us to evolve a distinctive methodology whose basic principle, as Dr. Faruqi points out, is the principle of the unity of truth. Truth, he observes, is a modality of God and is inseparable from Him. Reality derives its meaning and values from God's will. Its actuality has no meaning other than its fulfilment or unfulfilment of value. No social investigation, therefore, can be complete if it does not include its standing within the realm of ends. Moreover, Islam regards all values as 'society's stick'. They are socially related to and only obtained within the social order of the *Ummah*. That is why there is no concept of personal morality or piety which does not include social action. Thus Shari'ah attains an inviolable rank in human society. It cannot be violated without disturbing human personality both for its individual gain and its social function. In other words, religion has set a goal for man. He achieves this goal within the framework of his society in which he lives and has his being. The individual is thus seen in the context of his or her family and the family always is seen in the context of society and society in the context of the world of humanity on this earth. Human beings and the entire range of human activity as also the entire history of the human race are seen in the context of a cosmic order. This cosmic order involves not only life on this earth but also life after death. It is because of this that man has been granted a system for his progress towards the destiny that he deserves. If he lives according to that system he can become the vicegerent of God on earth. It is this system which provides society with basic fundamental laws of living known in the Islamic code as Shari'ah. These are absolute and unchangeable laws integrally related to the innate nature of man (*fitrah*). It is from this point of view too that Islam is a natural religion.

Environmental changes bring about social change but all these social changes are assessed and judged by Muslims with reference to Shari'ah, or that order which has been revealed to man from generation to generation through different prophets to the last prophet of Islam. In other words, social changes which contradict or challenge the basic laws are to be regarded by the Muslim sociologist as antagonistic to the basic nature of man. To try to analyze society without any reference to this order is to make that analysis goalless or extremely personal or subservient to some invented philosophy, whose assumptions are either unknown or known in an esoteric manner to an individual or to a few. Can man become a measure for man when we do not have any external norm to measure him by?

When we turn our attention to historical writings in the West we are again confronted with the same contradictions and shortcomings. Just as in the case of human society in general, Islam enjoins the historians also to discover the laws of nature rather than to invent new theories about human life. Events occurring in the past and in the present have a common law working behind them. Just as there is no change in the laws of nature, and it is the function of a scientist not to invent new laws but to find and express the laws operative in external nature, so also the historians are expected to build their assessments on the foundations provided by religion. From this point of view the Islamic view of history is universal. It does not describe the role of a few people or a chosen people, but it 'discusses the role of the entire humanity in its attitude towards truth and righteousness'.

The concept of history as it has developed in the West has serious shortcomings both from the philosophical point of view and from the point of view of its application to human life on earth. These shortcomings have been presented by Professor Abdul Hamid Siddiqi in his essay 'The Islamic Concept of History'. What he says is related to what we have stated earlier about the concept of social change. Because of the stress laid by modern philosophers on the impersonal and unconscious process that they think governs social changes, it has become almost impossible for historians to consider man as a free agent working within certain limits. Professor Abdul Hamid points out the common elements among the different concepts of history that are prevalent in the West. They are as follows: (a) the human ego is hemmed in by time and space and it enjoys no freedom of will; (b) the collective impersonal is alone real and the independent existence of the individual is an illusion; (c) man's destiny is entirely shaped by social forces and not by his inner being; (d) there is no eternal truth, no objective standard of morality and justice. All these concepts are relative to time and space, and thus there is no law and command that can be held to be universally true.

Islam on the other hand asserts that man's ego is free and hence his action is to be judged with reference to a code of morality. Besides this Islam also relates through the Quran, the past of humanity whose traces have not been discovered by modern historians such as the traces of civilizations that prevailed long before Judaic history started being written. The Quran refers to many incidents and situations which cannot be demonstrably determined but whose truth Muslims do not question. The very concept of first man on earth is untenable from the Western historical point of view. Similarly the idea that the first man on earth was a spiritually and morally highly developed personality contradicts the Western concept according to which man has evolved from primitivism to the modern civilized state. According to Islam, Adam did not know the instruments of civilization but morally and spiritually he was a highly cultured man, one who was endowed with essential knowledge about life and values. Moreover, the Islamic concept of history differentiates between culture that is dependent on values, and

80

civilization which is dependent mainly on the evolution of mechanisms. Historically, therefore, man has gone on piling up and refining these mechanisms or rather the instruments of civilization and thus making life more and more complex, but this has not gone on improving man's value consciousness. Man has not become a better man by going to the Moon. Islam judges historical events from a moral point of view. The Quranic concept of history makes us realize that the rise and fall of civilizations are integrally related to the rise and fall in value consciousness in these civilizations. The appearance of prophets on earth was thus intimately tied up with the growth and evolution of man's moral being in different areas where human life prevailed. The prophet would appear entrusted with the task of lifting man out of the quagmire of corruption. Sometimes nations were completely destroyed because of their rejection of the teachings of these prophets and sometimes, because of their acceptance, they made quick progress towards prosperity and happiness. Thus instead of history being a continuous process of evolution towards better and more complicated civilizations it is regarded in Islam as a process through which man continuously rises towards perfection but falls into corruption and is destroyed.

We notice the same attitude in the concepts of economics and political science which led to the segregation of the divine and the secular in the West in the sixteenth and seventeenth centuries. R. H. Tawney in his book *Religion and the Rise of Capitalism* has clearly described this process of secularization. As man is the measure of man, as society is considered to be evolving on its own and generating morality on the basis of social evolution, there is no transcendental norm. Therefore the science of economics has to be understood from the point of view of man's pursuit of self-interest in the sphere of production and distribution of wealth. Thus science has ignored the altruistic aspect of human nature, his fear of God, his love of Man and his awareness that he has to give an account of his deeds after death. Those who believe in these concepts and the society which is constituted of such people, have a different way of approaching wealth and organizing its production and distribution. Thus the concepts of property, freedom, competition and the role of the state are integrally related to the concept of man and his life in this world and in the world hereafter. Professor Mohammad Nejatullah Siddiqi, in his essay on 'The Teaching of Economics' at the University level in Muslim countries, indicates how both in capitalistic and socialistic economics there is no constructive programme of action which relates human life to a moral priority rooted in human attitudes. Both are highly mechanical. In a capitalist economy attention is focussed on the material and technical problem of maximum production and is oriented to individualism, exploitative capitalism and imperialism and it is strongly biased against a social and moral approach. Similarly, the Marxist approach replaces the market by the State as the mechanism for choice and makes man a passive agent not to be trusted with freedom. Neither of these, therefore, is Islamic in nature. According to the Islamic concept man's choice is considered to be influenced by his assessment of its possible consequences for society, by his fear of the consequences in after-life and by other social, cultural and political considerations. This broader concept of economic rationality needs detailed formulation by Muslim economists.

The same difficulty is visualized in the field of political science. A modern political scientist who is a Muslim is placed in a situation which is extremely difficult from the point of view of his belief and the translation of his faith into action. According to him there is a close relationship between authority granted by God and the good action of the *Ummah*. Moreover, *Ummah* is a concept that transcends geographical and political boundaries. Muslims wherever they be, belong to this *Ummah* and must owe their basic loyalty to it. The separation of church and state that we have witnessed in the evolution of Western thought and development, is not Islamic because in Islam from the very outset the need for the establishment of a political system was felt and put into operation. The spiritual and the temporal are not two distinct domains in Islam; political authority is intimately related to the necessity of enforcing the basic laws given to man in the Quran and the Sunnah. As Iqbal pointed out, 'the unity called man is body, when you look at it as acting in regard to what we call the external world; it is mind or soul when we look at it as acting in regard to the ultimate aim and ideal of such acting. The essence of *tawhid* as a working idea is equality, solidarity and freedom. The state, from the Islamic standpoint, is an endeavour to transform these ideal principles into space-time forces, an aspiration to realize them in a different human organization.'[11]

That is why a Muslim state is different from a nation state. The former organizes the entire system in order to realize a divine purpose in human life and enforce a divinely sanctioned law for human society. It directs its vision towards universal man and its goal towards Man's life in this world and in the hereafter, whereas in the latter, it is the interest of the nation that supersedes all other human interests, therefore sovereignty is ascribed to the nation instead of to God. Hence laws are evolved in the former with reference to an ideal unchanging pattern given by God and in the latter with reference to the needs of the society and, as the needs go on changing, laws are reformulated or altered or discarded as the case may be. Therefore, it is the perennial primordial tradition that governs the former and it is the temporal tradition that governs the latter. This concept is difficult to work out only because the concept of the nation-state has become widely prevalent in the modern world. People still think more in terms of belonging to one nation living within a geographical area than in terms of mankind unified by one law granted by God.

From the above discussion, it is evident that social sciences developed in the West have separated the worldly and spiritual interests of man. This separation is so deep that no relationship is established between the divinely sanctioned normal life and the norm evolved by man. That is why whereas in the case of Muslim social science the transcendent norm is applied and the moral and spiritual aspects of man's life are found integrally related to the mundane as well as to the spiritual according to modern social sciences, as developed in the West, we notice a complete denial of a God-granted norm and of absolute values geared to the production of the 'good'. In order to replace these concepts by the Islamic concepts of social sciences, Islamic thinkers have to go back to the past and also reformulate the concepts presented by past Muslim thinkers in the context of modern life. In this case the concept of man governed by self-interest or the interests of his nation will have to be replaced by a man whose primary concern is the good of others, i.e., the spiritual and moral benefits of man and hence the need for an organization in the economic and political and social fields which would help a man to flourish as a good man as conceived by the great religion. Muslim social thinkers have also to take into account the fact that the social order of an Islamic society is not a haphazard development. It imitates a body of principles or values that are known to have been revealed and of which the truth is taken for granted. Social institutions are the product of the application of metaphysical doctrines to contingent circumstances. The temporal or the local colour that they take go on changing with the times, but throughout they maintain a high degree of stability because these institutions are based on unchanging principles within a temporary context. Therefore they preserve a recognizable identity and go on continuously producing order from order.[12]

Natural Sciences: Integration versus Confrontation

When we turn our attention from the social sciences to the natural sciences, our difficulty in integrating modern scientific theories with Muslim theories of *tawhid* and revelation is the more acute because whereas in social sciences the assertion of the moral and spiritual aspects of man can be made, in the case of natural sciences the assertion of the divine and moral order does not become apparent to many thinkers. But the principle in both cases is exactly the same. Islam conceives an integrated relationship between external nature and man's own inner nature. It is the duty of man to understand and discover the original principles operative in the universe so that he may organize his own life in such a way that he may be able to utilize this knowledge for his own benefit. But man is not expected to change or alter the basic code of life. What has happened in modern science is the result of its ignoring or denying this code. The limits laid down by the code are clearly indicated in the way that man has to behave both with reference to the external world and with reference to his own society. Nature is not neutral. It reveals the divine purpose and therefore man is expected not to upset nature and forcibly redirect its energies in directions which are not normal. Genetic engineering, for example, is an attempt to have recourse to one aspect of natural law while ignoring the normal process asserted and sanctioned by divine law. Man himself does not know the consequences of such experiments and such an attempt to apply coercive methods on nature. Similary the social consequences of the scientific invention of birth control has led to the emergence of a new phenomenon known as permissiveness, which again is basically unnatural, irresponsible and hence anti-social. Its consequences are far-reaching and are resulting in the West in the destruction of the basis of society which is the family. Thus the philosophical stress on individualism has led to the denial of the basic natural law which is also the basis of humanity. We can therefore see the inter-relationship between scientific investigation and social consequences.

In a similar manner, we find the Western concept of confrontation between nature and man extremely unnatural. The Islamic concept is that of harmony between man and nature and not confrontation. To eliminate all the hills in order to create plain land to build a city, is to violate very seriously the natural order whose purpose has been stated very clearly in the Quran and the Sunnah. That would lead to a disharmony whose consequences we cannot foresee. If we therefore accept nature and the natural configuration of the land and build a city without disturbing that configuration arbitrarily, we can benefit from the ecological balance and the weather that is natural to that area. Thus the Islamic concept is to know the basic laws of the universe in order to be able to control it and to use it for one's benefit without disturbing or corrupting external nature.[13]

The other aspect of the teaching of science and technology is in the need for an integration of such teaching with the overall Islamic ideological pattern that prevails in society. The pattern of teaching technology and sciences in the West has recently been integrated into their ideological system. In America for example, as Dr. Waqar Hussaini has said, humanities and social sciences are taught within the framework of American culture, the Western ideologies of political democracy and capitalist economy and in general within the ethnocentric perspective of Judaeo-Christian Western civilization. Similarly, in Soviet Russia, scientific education is integrated with non-technical disciplines and all students are compelled to know the history of the Communist Party in the Soviet Union, Marxist ethics, Marxist-Leninist philosophy and aesthetics, fundamentals of scientific atheism, political economy and fundamentals of scientific communism. It is only in Muslim countries that this integration of ideology with techno-humanistic and techno-social disciplines has not taken place. This is the sphere in which much can be achieved if educators can formulate courses suitable for this type of education.

Extracts

1. Redefining Social Sciences

(i) Dr. Ismail Rajhi Faruqi: from *Islamicizing Social Sciences*

Dr. Ismail Rajhi Faruqi is Professor of Religion in Temple University, Philadelphia. He has edited *The Historical Atlas of World Religions*, and has written on different aspects of Islam especially in the context of the modern world. He clearly indicates the shortcomings of Western methodology and gives the concept of *Ummatic* sciences.

1. All learning whether it pertains to the individual or to the group, to man or to nature, to religion or to science, must reorder itself under the principle of tawhid, i.e., that Allah (*subhanna wa ta'ala*) exists and is one, and that He is the Creator, the Master, Provider, Sustainer, the ultimate metaphysical cause, purpose and end of everything that is. All

objective knowledge of the world is knowledge of His will, His arrangement, His wisdom. All human willing and striving is by His leave and permission. It ought to fulfil His command, the divine pattern He has revealed, if its is to earn for its subject happiness and felicity.

2. Pre-eminently, the sciences which study man and his relations with other humans ought to recognize man as standing in a realm dominated by God metaphysically as well as axiologically. These sciences include human history – the realm in which the higher levels of the divine pattern are to be realized. Properly speaking, they ought to be concerned with the Khilafah of God on earth, with man's vicegerency. And since man's vicegerency is necessarily social, the sciences that study it should properly be called Ummatic, Muslim learning repudiates the bifurcation, humanities/social sciences. It calls for re-classification of the disciplines into natural sciences dealing with nature, and *Ummatic* sciences dealing with man and society. If, in the Association of Muslim Social Scientists of America and Canada, we continue to call them social, we do so in defiance of the West which insists on separating them from the humanities. We must remember that the study of society cannot be free from judgement and valuation and is therefore subject to the same rigour, or absence of it, as philosophy, theology, law, literature and the arts. Conversely, the humanities are as much concerned with the ummah as the so-called social disciplines, and are capable of applying the same principles of validation to their materials and conclusions.

3. The Ummatic sciences should not be intimidated by the natural sciences. Their place in the total scheme of human knowledge is one and the same with the difference lying in the object of study, not the methodology. Both aim at discovering and understanding the divine pattern: the one in physical objects, the other in human affairs. Understanding the pattern in each realm certainly calls for different techniques and strategies, but in final analysis, i.e., as instantiations of the divine pattern, the two are subject to the same laws of verification. Apart from specification of rituals, description of the transcendent, and reportage about the unknown past, which may be difficult to subject to rational enquiry, nothing which Islam gave us by way of *naql* or tradition, is not as confirmed or confirmable by reason and understanding, as what we received or continue to discover by way of *'aql*. Nothing stands beyond the strategies of human comprehension.

4. The West claims that its social sciences are scientific because they are neutral; that they deliberately avoid human judgement and prefer-

ence; that they treat the facts as facts and leave them to speak for themselves. This, we have seen, is a vain claim. For there is no theoretical perception of any fact without perception of its axiological nature and relations. Hence, instead of withholding analysis of the axiological aspect which cannot be done anyway, and allowing axiological considerations to determine the conclusion surreptitiously, a genuine scientist will carry out *all* his analyses in the open. He will never claim to talk about human society when he is in fact referring to Western society, of religion when he is in fact referring to Christianity, or of social and economic laws when he is in fact referring to common practices of some Western societies.

5. Finally, Islamicization of the social sciences must endeavour to show the relation of the reality studied to that aspect or part of the divine pattern pertinent to it. Since the divine pattern is the norm reality ought to actualize, the analysis of what is should never lose sight of what ought to be. Moreover, the divine pattern is not only normative, enjoying a heavenly modality of existence removed from actuality. It is also real in the sense that Allah has predisposed reality to embody it, a kind of *fitra* existence which Allah, in His mercy, had implanted in human nature, in the human individual or group, in the Ummah as an ongoing stream of being, which moral action pulls out into actuality and history. Every scientific analysis would therefore endeavour, if it is Islamic, to expose this immanent divine pattern in human affairs, to underline that part of it which is *in actu*, and that part of it which is *in potentia*; to expose the factors realizing or impeding the completion of the process of embodiment, to focus the light of understanding upon the relations of that process to all the other processes of Ummatic life.

The Islamic social scientist is endowed with the cause of Islam. The divine pattern in human affairs is the object of his constant attention and care as well as hope and yearning. He is not only scientific in the sense of not leaving out the axiological aspects, but is pre-eminently critical of reality in light of the divine pattern.

Per contra, the Western social scientist cannot afford to be critical of the ultimate purposes or ends of society but only of the means thereto, because of his conscious commitment to description rather than advocacy. This commitment, however, was hardly ever honoured because his denial of the relevance of the spiritual was, in final analysis, a denial of relevance to Church-related values, and an assertion of relevance to utilitarian and cultural values which he honoured subjectively, in tribal or Protagorean fashion. The Islamic social scientist, on the other hand, has maintained an open and public commitment to the values of Islam, an ideology which lays a rational, critical claim to the truth. He is not afraid or ashamed of being corrected by his Muslim or non-Muslim peers, for the truth, in his view, is none other than the intelligent reading of nature in scientific report and experiment, or the reading of God's revelation in His holy book. God is the Author of both; and both of His works are public, appealing to no magisterium other than that of reason and understanding.

Under such view, the Islamic social scientist is capable of bringing a new critique to social science. Loyalty to means and instrumental ends has caused Western social science to degenerate into 'strategic studies', i.e., studies of strategies leading to goals, the validity of which nobody claims to be critically establishable. Through commitment to Islam, the social scientist is bound to regard man as God's vicegerent, whose duty is to actualize value in history. Islamic social science can therefore humanize the discipline and reinstate the *humanitas* ideal in the life of man, the being whom Western social science has taught to regard as helpless puppet of blind forces.

(ii) *The Meaning of History*
Professor Abdul Hamid Siddiqui: from *The Islamic Concept of History*

Professor Abdul Hamid Siddiqui was Professor of History in the Panjab University, Pakistan. He shows the incompatibility between Western and Islamic concepts and methodologies of history.

The Quran is not a book of History but it is a Divine Verdict on History. The superb style in which the Holy Quran has discussed the different phases of the lives of various nations – their rise, development and decline, as well as the causes underlying these changes – has no parallel in the historical records of the world. It was under the impact of the Quran that man learnt to furnish answers to the two fundamental questions 'Why it happened' and 'How it happened', and he began to fight against the conception of 'chance' as the motive force of change in the universe and strove to discover the determining law of which what man calls 'chance' is the visible expression. Thus, the transition from mere narration of events to their rational explanation and the introduction of logical order in their records, all these developments in human history are due to the Holy Quran. That the Divine Book narrates the events of the past as *'Ibra* (instructive value) is because events occurring in the past and in the present have meaningful relations between them, or in other words, they have a common law working behind them. Just as there is no change in the laws of Nature, and the physical phenomena of our age are controlled by those very laws which governed them in the past, so is the case with the human race and its problems. The passions and pleasures and the political and domestic problems of the peoples of those remote ages were, in all likelihood, much the same as ours, since the psychic make-up of all human beings is identical. The Islamic view of History is universal; it is neither time-bound nor space-bound. It does not examine the role of a 'chosen people' only, but also discusses the role of entire humanity in its attitude towards truth and righteousness.

Further, the Quran and the Sunnah have brought into prominence the role of man as a free agent working within certain limits. The philosophers and historians of the modern age have been unduly stressing the deep, impersonal, unconscious processes that govern social changes. They have accordingly tended to minimize the power of ideas and ideals, or have even denied this power altogether. The complexities that make it difficult for them to ascertain the law of social change also strengthen their erroneous impression that man has no real freedom to make his history. It is under this false impression that various theories of social change have been evolved and propounded. Philosophers like Spengler look upon culture, which is another name for man-made environment, as an organism governed by the biological laws of life and death. He, in his craze to depersonalize History, seized upon the outer manifestations of culture for building up the hypothesis, but ignored the inner dominating human force working behind it. . . .

Islam exhorts a Muslim to see not only the outward manifestation of the different happenings of human life, but to study the undercurrent of ideals and motives which have shaped those happenings. The historical references and the accounts of the past are given in the Quran not so much to fill in the gaps of our factual knowledge, but to systematize and generalize the past and to take lessons from it. The Holy Quran treats events of the past not only with a view to reviving them in our memory but to making them meaningful and instructive to us. It selects significant events, interprets them in the light of moral law, and then evaluates them according to ethical judgements; and in the whole process of selecting, interpreting and evaluating the facts, it provides answers to the crucial questions about the destiny of mankind. . . .

The Holy Quran and the Hadith have urged us to review past events, both reported and experienced, as indications that they should awaken in us a strong moral sense and at the same time enhance our ability to act according to the Commands of God, to penetrate into the apparently meaningless succession of events and discern the ever-present Design and Will of the Creator and perceive that all being and happening in the world is the outcome of a conscious, all-embracing Power; and unless one is in spiritual accord with the demands of that Power, one cannot fulfil the Divine purpose for which one has been sent to this world.

2. Science and Religion: Integrated Courses of Studies

(i) *To integrate science and technology with the ideology and cultural ethos of Islam and Islamic ethics and ideology with humanities and social sciences.* Dr. Sayyid Waqar Ahmed Husaini: from *Humanistic-social sciences studies in High Technical Education: Islamic and international perspectives and the programme at College of Engineering King Abdulaziz University.*

Dr. Sayyid Waqar Ahmed Husaini, Associate Professor, College of Engineering, King Abdulaziz University, Jeddah, Saudi Arabia whose publications include *Principles of Environmental Engineering Systems Planning in Islamic Culture* and *Law, Politics, Economics, Education and the Sociology of Science and Culture*, proposes a method of integrating Islamic Culture courses with natural science subjects at the University level in order to make education Islamic in character and impact.

The prerequisites for contemporary rejuvenation of Islamic civilization are the restoration of Islamic humanistic-social sciences studies in technical education, and the restoration of the study of natural sciences and technology in humanistic-social sciences specializations: particularly in the faculties of Shari'ah and Islamic Studies as the Faculty of Humanities and Arts, and the Faculty of Shari'ah and Islamic Studies should be one and the same.

The restoration of the integrity of the education system through introduction of the two components in each, in proper proportion, is an Islamic epistemological necessity. One cannot be ignorant or independent of the *ayat Allah* in either natural sciences and technology or in humanities and social sciences. This is the essence of the 'Two-Book' concept in the Quran, of revelation of God's will.

The Objectives and Goals of Humanistic-Social Sciences Studies

Humanistic-social sciences studies, and their ideological orientation towards Islam, must have the following major objectives:

1. The development in thought and deed of the personal and social ethics of Islam for a successful life in this world and hereafter;

90

2. the appreciation of the social, economic, political, cultural, philosophical, national, developmental, and similar factors in the analysis of scientific-technological problems and solutions;

3. the understanding of our national and regional social environment, and our micro-biosphere, which influence, and are influenced by, science and technology;

4. the development of personal and group attitudes and abilities that enable people to give their technical education and training, and research and development efforts, a situational orientation; that is, the focus on personal application, development, field and practical work relevant for solving national and regional developmental problems;

The above two objectives require originality and resourcefulness, i.e., an innovative mentality (*ijtihadiyya*) and the creatively imitative (*taqlidiyya*). Mentality, which are distinct from pure or blind imitation (*taqlid mahd*). This will enable our scientists and technologists to make the right application of technology. The consequences of misapplication of modern technology are all too obvious in the developing countries. We ought to be able to learn from the self-criticism in industrialized societies that has been inspired by the growing recognition of the environmental crisis.

5. the self-realization of the historical and contemporary behavioural cultural patterns of Muslims which caused the decline, and are causing the retardation, of our scientific and technological development; and the self-realization of those ideal cultural patterns of Islam, historically manifested in the Muslim civilization of the first to fifth Hijri centuries (seventh to eleventh Christian centuries), which developed the most superior system of science and civilization. This objective is also intended to inculcate the Islamic rational or scientific method so that science and technology become something willed from within our self and our cultural ethos. They should not remain, as they do now, an extraneous appendage and an artificial civilization with no links with men's minds and their social behaviour.

The basic goals of these objectives are:

(a) to integrate science and technology with the ideology and cultural ethos of Islam, and to place them in the perspective of the history and sociology of Muslim science and technology; and

(b) to integrate Islamic ethics and ideology with humanities and social sciences, and to give these too a sense of continuity in the history of Islamic thought.

Chapter Five

The Disciplined Muse or the Muse Licentious?

The Creative Process

The Humanities, which include literature and fine arts, and philosophy, fall into the category of acquired knowledge along with social and natural sciences. In spite of this similarity, there is a fundamental difference between the two branches of knowledge. Whereas in social and natural sciences there is an attempt to find out and assess both external nature and Human society without trying to express the writer's own emotive reaction to his findings, in a work of art the writer is compelled to proceed to the realization of truth through an analysis of his emotive response to the world. In the former there is no attempt to create a fictitious world whereas in the latter the whole means of realizing truth is through some fiction, that is, something which is not actual but which represents the universal. Fiction plays, therefore, a very important role in this creative activity.

Fiction by itself would be meaningless if the author did not realize the truth that the fiction should symbolize. Even this realization goes through a process of imaginative analysis of the reality that the writer has emotionally responded to. But here again there is a necessity to understand the absolute and the contingent.[1] If a writer fails to do so it will not be possible for him to represent the universal. Unfortunately today in the West, the central basic concept of universality is lost sight of in the midst of all kinds of individualism. Whereas previously in the West itself the artist was thought to imitate the intellectual or formal nature of things, today he is asked to emphasize only the aesthetic aspect. The archetypal world[2] which is imitated in traditional art is forgotten in modern concepts.

Islam, like other religions, demands that the artist or the writer should try to imitate the intellectual or the formal nature of things after having submitted himself to the self-discipline which his religion demands. How can his imagination get a glimpse of ultimate truth if his self is vitiated by narrow prejudices or partial eccentricities or self-made philosophy? The response to the ultimate can only come and be accurately felt and realized when the self is purified enough to get the reflection of that reality. As long as the self is governed by the poet's or the artist's own worldly inclinations, as long as he does not submit to the Almighty and purify his vision, would it not be possible for his self to respond to that truth which is beyond his narrow self. In other words, religious discipline releases the Muse from the bonds of narrow self-interest and selfish passions.[3] The soul becomes free to respond to any situation from a spiritual point of view and thus realize what Plotinus called 'that archetypal world . . . the true golden age, the age of Kronos, an intellectual principle as being the offspring or exuberance of God'.[4] It is only then that we become aware of the turmoil in the temporal in its true perspective and try to put it in a form that at once transcends naturalistic art and penetrates into that which is in the nature of things.

The Tower of Babel

The difficulty that the modern reader faces lies basically in this individualistic perception of reality and secondly in the formulation of an esoteric philosophy on the basis of this partial realization. The writer's or the artist's job is not to give a new philosophy of life but to give his own realization of truth about life. But in order to realize that truth he has to proceed through life with some instrument to measure accidents and events. But when a writer discards a basic view of life and the laws of existence and behaviour which religion has taught him, he is bound to create difficulties for the reader and bound to influence him in different directions. This is the greatest problem that a modern reader faces when he reads modern literature. Either he is confronted with a philosophy or he is led to believe that the realization of the writer is final and true.

The reader or the viewer is thus confronted with several concepts which sometimes contradict each other but in each case there is a departure from perennial tradition. They therefore make the reader forget the archetypal world in the world of changing patterns. This also affects the manners of expression of different kinds of art and literature and leads to the production of that kind of work in which fictionality is dissociated from a deeper realization of truth. A reader is expected to suspend his beliefs and accept or be moved by the writer's representation of the world as he sees it. As each individual writer has his own way of seeing reality, each of these visions is highly particular, narrow and hence partial. Writers have gone to the extent of inventing moral codes and representing them through fiction and poetry and drama and even in art forms. This creates multiplicity without unity and hence confuses the reader. Either he will have to give up his beliefs in order to accept any single point of view or he will be influenced by many points of view without being able to realize where the ultimate truth lies. This is what has been characterized by a modern critic as a Tower of Babel.[5] According to the Muslim concept which is also universally acceptable to all basic religions, there is no need for a writer to invent any philosophy or morality in order to appreciate human life and present it through his writings. He can accept the normal natural moral philosophy which is common to all important religions of the world and try to realize human life through that norm. That norm itself becomes a part of himself and goes beyond being just an intellectually accepted scheme of values when he emotionally responds to human life and the external world and enters the deeper realms of moral values. Thus the values become experiential reality. This way of looking at literature and fine arts is lacking in modern criticism and hence the choice of classics in the teaching of literature has become very difficult. In the name of freedom from religious and moral restraints, a large number of Western writers have given complete licence to the Muse. That is why it has become difficult to choose between the right and the wrong, good and bad, eternal and temporal, universal and particular. The person, therefore, educated in literature and fine arts can become, in the words of Newman, 'a gentleman' with fine sensibility but not necessarily a religious man with pure sensibility.[6] If education is a means of creating that personality whose basic approach to life is to be governed by inspired intellectual activity and emotive realization of truth, then it becomes necessary that the basic norm of values inherent in religion should be kept in view and should not be allowed to disintegrate through the advocacy of that critical approach which upholds individualism and undermines religious conscience.

Fine Arts: The Traditional vis-à-vis the Naturalistic

So far as the basic approach is concerned all traditional arts including literature and fine arts both in the East and the West express this idea.

94

Whether it is Plato or St. Augustine or St. Thomas Aquinas or Islam or the Uparistadas, the fundamental idea is not to imitate or describe external nature but, in the words of Titus Burkhardt an extract from whose article follows, 'to endow all objects by which man naturally surrounds himself – a house, a fountain, a drinking vessel, a garment, a carpet – with the perfection each object can possess according to its own nature. . . .' Islamic art does not add something alien to the objects it shapes, it only brings forth their potential qualities. This is exactly what is meant in the Judaic tradition as we find in *Exodus* 25:40 in which God instructs Moses regarding the building of the temple and its furniture, 'And look that thou make them after their pattern, which was shewed thee in the mount.' Plato means the same thing when he speaks of the construction of the *polis*, 'The city can never otherwise be happy unless it is designed by those painters who follow a divine original'.[7] Plotinus expands this idea and says, 'In contemplative vision, especially when it is vivid, we are not aware of our personality, we are in possession of ourselves, but the activity is towards the object of vision with which the speaker becomes identified; he has made himself over as matter to be shaped; he takes ideal form under the action of the vision, while remaining potentially himself.'[8] St. Thomas Aquinas further differentiates between God's work and the work of the artist who identifies himself with the nature of the object, 'God is the cause of things made by His intellect and will, just as the craftsman is the cause of the things made by his craft'.[9] 'Now the knowledge of the artificer is the cause of things made by his art from the fact that the artificer works through his intellect. Hence the form in the intellect must be the principle of action.'[10] According to this traditional concept then the true artist would try to understand and embody in his work the real or essential forms of things.

The naturalistic art, that has practically replaced this traditional art in the West, insists on imitating not the idea but the external form. There is of course an attempt to universalize through the particular but the central theme has become the image of Man as the artist sees it. Hence the artist relies more on his experience of the external factual world, on actuality, than on his internal realization of the ideal, the universal, the eternal dimension of that external world. He does not try to imitate the idea and symbolize it as a traditionalist would do.

For Muslim readers and thinkers, there is an additional difficulty. Muslims do not believe in figurative representation of reality because they feel that in painting, architecture, decorative art and such other forms of art, the representation of truth by figures restricts the imagination of the reader to the world of appearances in spite of the representation being extremely formal. It is the concept of *tawhid* or unity of God that permeated Muslim art in its early stages and that was why calligraphy, arabesques and such other abstract designs and architectural patterns, became so important for the Muslim artist. Thus a Muslim artist was expected to go beyond any semblance of external forms and create abstract symbols representing Eternal Beauty and thus take the reader or viewer with him into that stage of consciousness which makes him feel the pulse of Eternity. Even to confine one's attention to an extremely formal representation of an idea or an attribute of God through a figure, restricts the attention of the viewer to one quality or one idea and he is often misled into thinking that to be representative of the whole truth, whereas truth in the comprehensive sense is God, who is beyond all attributes and hence beyond all forms. That is why beauty is expected not to be confined to certain figures but to be represented through some abstract designs which immediately take the mind beyond the natural forms manifested in the universe to that which is beyond the form. But the invasion of the Western theories of naturalistic art is now undermining this traditional concept and thus diverting the attention of the artist, from the representation of beauty in the abstract, to an imitation of beauty in the particular.

The following extracts have been chosen to illustrate these ideas and also point out that the modernization of Muslim society has led to the acceptance of the Western naturalistic version of Reality and it is felt that the Muslim mind is going to be invaded by the same multifarious and conflicting concepts of Man and his destiny that have affected the Western mind.

Extracts

1. *The Role of Fine Arts in Muslim Education*

(i) *Essence of Islamic art vis-à-vis that of modern European art and its place in Muslim Education.*
   Titus Burckhardt: from *The role of Fine Arts in Muslim Education*

Ibrahim Ezzuddin Titus Burckhardt who embraced Islam in 1934 while in Fez, Morocco, is an eminent authority on Muslim art and has also made an intensive study of Islamic doctrines including Sufism. Since 1972 he has been working as a UNESCO expert for the preservation of the cultural legacy of Fez. His publications include *Art of Islam, Language and Meaning, An Introduction to Sufi Doctrine, Moorish Culture in Spain, Sacred*

Art in East and West. He finds a close relationship between the ideal Islamic way of life and Islamic Art and points out the significance of those elements in the preservation and furtherance of Islamic culture.

The European conception of art and its conception in the world of Islam are different to the point that one may ask whether the common use of such words as 'art' and 'artist' does not create more confusion than mutual understanding. Almost everything in European art is image. Consequently the highest rank in the hierarchy of European arts is held by figurative painting and sculpture. These are 'free arts', whereas architecture as conditioned by technical necessities occupies a lower rank. Even 'lower' are the 'decorative' arts. From the European point of view, the criterion of an artistic culture lies in its capacity to represent nature and even more in its capacity to portray man. From the Islamic point of view, on the contrary, the main scope of art is not imitation or description of nature – man's work will never equal God's art – but the shaping of human ambience. Art has to endow all objects by which man naturally surrounds himself – a house, a fountain, a drinking vessel, a garment, a carpet – with the perfection each object can possess according to its own nature. The perfection of a building for instance depends on three dimensional geometry, according to the perfection of the crystalline state of matter, while the art of the carpet involves two dimensional geometry as well as the harmony of colours. Islamic art does not add something alien to the objects it shapes, it only brings forth their potential qualities. It is essentially objective; in fact, neither the research of the most perfect profile for a cupola nor the rhythmical display of a linear ornament have much to do with the personal mood of an artist. . . . The Muslim artist, by his very Islam, his surrender to the Divine law, is always aware of the fact that it is not he who produces or invents beauty, but that a work of art is beautiful to the degree that it obeys the cosmic order and therefore reflects universal beauty, *Al-hamdu lillah wahdah*. This awareness, if it excludes promethean attitudes, by no means diminishes the joy of artistic creativity; as the works themselves testify, it confers on Islamic art a serene and somehow impersonal character. For the Muslim mind, art reminds it of God when it is as impersonal as are the laws that govern the movement of the heavenly spheres.

As is well known, the Islamic negation of anthropomorphic art is both absolute and conditional: it is absolute with regard to all images which could be an object of worship, and it is conditional with regard to art forms imitating living bodies. We refer to the saying of the Prophet who condemned artists who try to 'ape' the creation of God: in their after-life they will be ordered to give life to their works and will suffer from their incapacity to do so. This *hadith* has been interpreted in different ways; in general, it was understood as the condemnation of an intrinsically blasphemous intention, and therefore Islam tolerates anthropomorphic art forms on condition that they do not create the illusion of living beings; in miniature painting, for instance, central perspective suggesting three-dimensional space has been avoided. . . .

The central theme of European art and – we might also say – the central theme of Christian art, is the image of man. In Islam too, man is the centre to which all arts refer, but as a rule he is not himself a theme of visual art. If we consider the general Islamic reluctance against figurative art or against anthropomorphic art in all its depth, we discover a tremendous respect for the divine origin of the human form. The same is true, in a way, of traditional Christian art, but the consequences, on both sides, are entirely different. . . .

Essence of Islamic Art and its place in education

The essence of art is beauty, and beauty is by its very nature an exterior as well as an interior reality. According to a well-known saying of the Prophet, 'God is beautiful and He loves beauty' (*Allahu jamilun – wayuhibbul – jamal*). Beauty therefore is a divine quality (*sifatun ilahiya*) reflecting itself in whatsoever is beautiful on earth. Some scholars perhaps will object that beauty mentioned in that Hadith is of a purely moral character, but there is no reason why we should limit the import of this prophetical word, nor why Divine Beauty should not shine forth on every level of existence.

No doubt Divine Beauty is incomparable, exalted above physical as well as above moral beauty, but at the same time nothing beautiful can exist outside the dominion of that divine quality: 'God is beautiful and He loves beauty;' this means He loves His own reflection in the world.

According to a number of famous Muslim metaphysicians, Divine beauty (*jamal*) includes all the divine attributes expressing bounty and grace or the merciful irradiation of God in the world, whereas Divine Majesty (*jalal*) includes all the divine attributes of severity, which in a way manifest the transcendent nature of God with regard to His creation. More generally speaking each divine quality contains all the other ones, for they all refer to one single essence. Therefore beauty implies Truth (*haqq*), and vice-versa, Truth implies beauty. There is no real beauty unless Truth is concealed in it, and there is no real Truth unless beauty emanates from it. This reciprocal character of universal qualities has its reflection on the level of traditional teaching, and in this connection it has been said, 'in Islam art is a science and science is an art'. This word directly refers to the geometrical lore involved in Islamic art, a lore which allows the artist to develop harmonious forms from fundamental geometrical patterns. In a higher meaning, however, art is a science because it opens a way to contemplative knowledge whose ultimate object is Divine Beauty, and science is an art in so far as it is oriented towards unity and therefore possesses a sense of equilibrium or harmony which lends it a kind of beauty.

Modern European art, whatever occasional beauties it may possess, is generally enclosed within the particular psychic world of its author; it contains no wisdom, no spiritual grace. As for modern science, it neither possesses nor demands any beauty; being purely analytic, it scarcely opens the eyes for a contemplative sight of things. When it studies man, for instance, it never contemplates his entire nature which is at once body, soul and spirit. If we make modern science responsible for modern technology, it is at the very basis of a whole world of ugliness. The least we can say is that modern science, in spite of all its learning and experience, is an unwise science. Perhaps the greatest lesson traditional Islamic art can teach us, lies in the fact that beauty is a criterion of truth: if Islam were a false religion, if it were not a divine message but a system invented by a man, could it have produced so many works of art endowed with everlasting beauty?

Here is the point where we pose the question: 'What should be the role of fine arts in Muslim education today?' The study of Islamic art, if undertaken with an open mind and without the European prejudices we have mentioned, is a way of approaching the spiritual background of the whole Islamic culture. The same is true for all traditional art.

2. Principles and Methods of Teaching Literature

(i) *Literature as a form of Knowledge*
Dr. Syed Ali Ashraf: from *Principles and methods of teaching Literature*

Dr. Syed Ali Ashraf, Professor of English, King Abdulaziz University, Jeddah, and Secretary of the Follow-up Committee, First World Conference on Muslim Education, looks at literature from the Islamic point of view and suggests some concrete methods of tackling the problem of choosing correct texts and of following the right method of teaching them.

Literature is a form of knowledge. This knowledge is partial but sincere and genuine. It is partial because it is only an individual's experience of reality. As that individual is a human being, his experience can never be complete. Only Allah has complete knowledge. But as experience is continually expanding this knowledge is also continually advancing and expanding. This expansion of knowledge means a continual recreation of Self because knowledge of anything other than Self is a means of making anything other than Self a part of one's Self. It is through this self-awareness that man becomes conscious of his relationship with God, with nature and with the world at large. It is within this Self that the essence of Man lies hidden, the essence about which Allah has said, 'I have breathed within him from my own spirit.'

But the awareness of this reality is not easily accessible to any individual because of the nature granted to man by Allah. On the one hand Allah has created man in the best possible image (*ahsan-i-taqweem*) and given him divine essence (*wana-fakhtufihe min ruhee*). On the other hand He has placed man in the world of matter and given him a passionate soul attached to his body (*nafs-i-ammara*) which tempts him towards the lowest of low regions (*asfala safeleen*). The great evil power – Satan – has not been stopped by Allah from trying to tempt man from the path of righteousness. Thus man is constantly in conflict within himself and with forces surrounding him. Therefore, the norm of righteousness revealed to man by Allah through his chosen Prophets (peace be upon them) can be responded to by the divine essence which is within man. At the same time the norm of selfishness, which evil powers within himself and outside him tempt him to accept for his temporary gain in this world, creates a conflict in his mind. It is this conflicting situation that attracts the writer's attention. He realizes how complex this conflict is. Imagination (*kheyal*) is that faculty within man which helps him to see the inter-relationship among various experiences and perceptions. It also synthesizes his perceptions and thus enables him to see the unity that exists behind the apparently divided and fragmented universe. Thus man's different senses bring different kinds of perceptions when he sees or perceives, for example, a table. But he is able to think of the table as a unit only because his imagination has helped him to unify his perceptions of colour, shape, form and touch and give to his mind the concept of a unified object. This concept of unity is ultimately derived from the concept of divine unity (*tawhid*) which the divine power within man makes him realize. Poetic imagination is the creative ability which helps man to break the rigid time and space association that memory imposes upon the series of experiences that man acquires and to recreate a new world out of the world of experiences in order to give to readers a beautiful image through which his vision of reality is expressed.

100

In other words, imagination is that faculty within man's Self which establishes the relationship between the Spirit and Self and hence between spiritual and material existence. Therefore it enables man to re-integrate sense and perceptions, intellectual formulations and spiritual realizations into new wholes and thus present his own image in different forms and colours. Imagination must be regarded, therefore, as a unifying factor. Only when this is accepted intellectually can one formulate critical principles in order to evaluate literature and indicate which is great and which is significant, which is good, which is bad. The difficulty that twentieth century writers are faced with is the difficulty brought about by the lack of faith in anything spiritual. Man stands disintegrated; that is why some important writers have tried to re-integrate man by reformulating his concepts and by establishing man's nature in a new context. This is what Ezra Pound or Yeats or D. H. Lawrence has tried to do. But the difficulty lies in the esotericism of these writers and their inability to see that they are trying to create various kinds of disconnected concepts. Their partial realizations are marred by their claim to have realized the whole.

It is of course true that even those who are not fully aware of their own faith in divine reality can create good literature provided they accept the basic conflict between Good and Evil presented in religion. It is from this moral framework of values that different writers draw sustenance. The genuineness and truthfulness of this realization depends on the writer's acceptance of the framework. This acceptance of the framework is always at first an intellectual or a social habit. A writer goes on understanding emotionally the significance of this framework and making it a part of his Self through the stress and strain of life where he has to take decisions and make choices.

Thus he grows and the morality grows within him. A great writer has therefore the humanity to realize various possibilities and choices and the possibility of modified perceptions and realizations. Every moment is a new start. But only when there is a final goal and a supreme framework can this start indicate progress, achievement, expansion and realization. Otherwise he may go round and round without any direction. Islam provides us with a final goal for Man. No higher and greater goal has ever been conceived. With this goal in view and with the ethical code that enables man to practise and grow through knowledge and action, the writer can proceed towards a new destiny and ever new realizations.

(ii) Methods of teaching literature: literature and values

In order to teach literature effectively as literature and at the same time teach it as a means of moral and spiritual training of students, our basic need is that of a scheme of literary criticism whose tenets are perfectly compatible with the concept of man which Islam provides. No writer can ever escape from his realization, however unconscious that may be, of what man is. It is only when he tries to conceive man in his own way and formulates a dogma that he comes into conflict with religious ideals, because his realization is bound to be extremely personal and hence limited. That is why it becomes necessary for literary critics to have a concept of Good and Evil. Basically it has never been difficult to have this concept, mainly because there is a universal recognition of certain values according to which man is judged. Islam has always claimed that there is only one religion in the universe, therefore there has always been one basic universal code of morality, of Good and Evil. As literature is primarily concerned with human life on this earth it is this universal code which literary criticism has to refer to in order to make students realize what is good literature and what is bad literature. . . .

The teacher of literature must therefore play the role of the critic. He has to discern the depth of writing according to the ability of the writer to go beyond the superficial, the social and individual circumstances, and penetrate into the realms of reality. He has to remove the temporary garments of personal prejudices, esoteric dogma and partial metaphysics and see naked Truth about humanity. No writer can have a complete knowledge of this Truth hence no critic can claim such completeness for anyone. Nor can a writer demand that his dogma or metaphysics can be accepted by any reader. As a critic the teacher has to see how far esoteric dogma or metaphysics is colouring the vision of the writer, how far the writer's emotive response to the human situation is governed by his day-to-day conventions and customs, and how far the writer has succeeded in concentrating his attention on the essential, universal problem which is surrounded by socio-cultural accretions, or which has got its peculiar slant and complexity because of contemporary socio-cultural conditions. . . .

The best method that the teacher can adopt in order to save students from being influenced by one author or the other is to make students proceed through the works of different writers who are at variance with each other. The teacher and students can then objectively explore the moral frameworks of different writers and find how conflicting their judgements and realizations are. At the same time it will be a highly instructive exploration for students if they are trying to find out how in spite of the variety of realizations these writers have been able to present truthful images about Man in various situations.

Chapter Six

The Teacher and the Taught

The Position of the Teacher: Traditional vis-à-vis Modern

The position of the teacher in modern society is vitally different from the place accorded to him in Islam. The teacher today is looked upon as a mere functionary who draws a salary either from the State or from a private organization and has certain specific responsibilities to discharge. His duties end with these responsibilities and he is seldom expected to go beyond them. Call it what you like, commercialism or modernization, the result of the change has been to create a kind of distance between the teacher and the taught and to eliminate the bonds, invisible but very real, which existed in practically all ancient societies, between them. The teacher in these societies, as in Islamic society, was more than a mere functionary. He was a model to be emulated.[1] He was expected to treat his charges not as so many sheep or cattle which needed to be herded or disciplined, but as impressionable human beings whose characters were to be moulded and who were to be initiated by him into the moral code which society cherished. For this reason in Islam the teacher was required not only to be a man of learning but also to be a person of virtue, a pious man whose conduct by itself could have an impact upon the minds of the young. It was not only what he taught that mattered; what he did, the way he conducted himself, his deportment in class and outside, were all expected to conform to an ideal which his pupils could unhesitatingly accept.

This conception of the teacher has unfortunately been undermined by modern changes. One could never dream in the old days of teachers going on strike, or either collectively or individually doing anything which might harm the interests of their pupils. Not only this, the teacher was looked up to, in Hindu society for instance, as a guru who instead of receiving payment from the pupils, maintained them until they had completed their education. A similar ideal was followed in Islam. The ancient seats of learning in Islam grew up around certain personalities who attracted pupils by reason alike of their learning and their piety. This had wide repercussions. It helped to communicate from one generation to the other the moral ideals which society valued. It helped to sustain and strengthen the foundations of ethics and it set before the young a model of virtue which they could unquestioningly follow. The result was a network of harmonious relationships which rendered social life smooth, which was an insurance against crime and which enabled society to move forward from age to age without serious disturbance or disruption. This is what is lacking in modern times. As the teacher comes to be looked upon more and more as a mere salaried person the pupils lose their respect for him as a man who deserves to be emulated and on whom they could model themselves. The teacher for his part has come to think that his responsibilities do not extend beyond what he does within the precincts of the school. Outside the classroom he is an ordinary individual without any special relationship with those whom he teaches.

The effects of this new relationship are felt acutely at all stages; they begin to be noticed very clearly as soon as one comes to deal with adolescents. This is one of the factors to which we must attribute the failure of many educational experiments. If children or young persons do not acquire as much as one would expect them to from what is taught to them, we must begin enquiring why this is happening and whether a return to the old system is possible or would be a cure for the ills which are so much in evidence today. Muslim thinkers are all agreed that the change from the old system to the new has been a change for the worse. It is recognized that quantitative changes in the size of schools or Universities do render it difficult for close personal relationships between the teacher and the taught, to grow. But the question which needs to be faced squarely is whether such large institutions are any good at all when the education they impart formally is negated by the deterioration in moral values, which results from the lack of personal bonds between the teacher and the taught.

As a matter of fact things have gone so far that nowadays when considering the qualifications of the teacher one does not think that his character demands any consideration at all. A teacher can be a morally degraded person but as long as he possesses the academic qualifications which entitle him to an appointment, it is felt that he should not be discriminated against.[2] The outcome, of course, can be imagined. Many institutions, schools and colleges, are today staffed by people who, whatever their academic qualifications, could by no stretch of the imagination be considered models of virtue. Quite the contrary indeed. This has two kinds of effect; the students either imbibe wrong habits from the teacher or begin to despise him. In either case, they find themselves caught in a serious dilemma. If they start copying evil habits from the teacher they develop a feeling of guilt and they gradually grow morally insensitive. If they, because of the home background, learn to despise the teacher for his conduct it limits what they can learn from him academically because pupils cannot possibly respond fully to someone whom in the depths of their hearts they despise. Whether the subject taught is philosophy or mathematics or physics, the pupil will always have the feeling that what is being given him is something tainted with evil, which before it was thoroughly assimilated would need to be examined with great care.

Student-Teacher Relationships Today

Whether the pupil articulates these feelings or not is immaterial. Deep within his mind there will be at work most of the time unconsciously a continual cross-examination. It is only occasionally that this might surface. But undoubtedly the contempt he would feel for the teacher would narrow the teacher's usefulness to him. This leads on to the fundamental question – what is education supposed to do? If it is agreed that education is not merely transmission of a body of information and that it includes also the training of men for life, then obviously the character of the teacher is a matter of paramount importance. This ideal was upheld in the heyday of Islam and it is to this, no matter what altered circumstances Muslim societies function in, that they should try to return. But how is this to be brought about?

We have seen before how in modern commercialized societies the relationship between the teacher and the taught has acquired an impersonal complexion. This we presume is the greatest danger which needs to be faced immediately. As long as the teacher continues to be a kind of faceless person, that is a functionary without a warm personality who does not respond emotionally to the needs of his pupils, he is more or less useless. So in addition to the right kind of text-book, and the right kind of training, we must also insist that the teacher should possess a warm personality to which young people can respond enthusiastically.

The personalities of the past whose names are cherished in Muslim history as great teachers have all been men possessed of warmth, who could immediately attract round them an ever-widening circle of learners, who learnt more from what they saw and heard than from what they read with them. The result was that even after the learners left their teachers' homes, or the schools or universities they attended, they continued to keep alive in their hearts and minds the memory of the great personalities with whom they had been in contact during a formative period of their lives.

This is a fact which nowadays is often overlooked. All the emphasis in the contemporary world is on buildings, tools, materials, equipment, rather than on the personality and character of the teacher. We believe that this should be the central issue which reformers must try and tackle. Once we have the right kind of men in the teaching profession, most of the problems will just vanish.

Teacher Education: Curricula and Methodology

Obviously much depends upon the training which the teacher himself receives. This underlines the vital importance in any scheme of educational reform of the role of teacher training institutions. Their syllabuses and curricula need to be reviewed in the light of the problem we have stated. There is very little at present being done to train teachers to be a kind of missionary but it must be recognized that unless the teacher is fired by a sense of mission, and unless he is prepared to accept a moral standard which society can admire and applaud, he will be a failure as a guide and as a model. In the context of Muslim society the teacher has to be a person deeply committed to Islam, not only outwardly but inwardly. He must be a virtuous person, a man of piety who considers it his responsibility to train his pupils to be good Muslims above all, that is to say, men and women who will learn the value of the Islamic moral code, who will in their lives live in accordance with the ethic which the Quran teaches, whose own conduct will be a pattern that the young can draw upon. The selection of such teachers may prove difficult but we are convinced that unless the old moral relationship between the teacher and the taught can be re-established, educational reforms will be a waste of time. We might produce good architects or good engineers or good scientists but would fail to produce good men and our society would have the social maladjustments which have bedevilled modern societies everywhere.

Dr. Hossein Nasr, Dr. Baloch, Dr. Aroosi and Dr. Badawi who have discussed this question arrive at the same conclusions: firstly, that the central pivot of any system of education is the teacher; secondly, that the teacher must be not only a man of learning but also a man of sterling moral worth; thirdly, that he must be a man with a sense of mission capable of inspiring in those with whom he comes in contact an enthusiasm for the moral and ethical code which he preaches and which he also exemplifies; fourthly, that he must be a person who teaches what he believes in. There must be no contradiction between the instruction he offers and his private beliefs. This last point has ruined the work of many teachers whose conduct was admirable. This has been due to the fact that teachers committed to the ethic of Islam sometimes find themselves teaching from books reflecting a different kind of morality and since they have not been trained how to tackle such a situation, they resort to a kind of double standard or neutrality in the classroom, elucidating the text-book in front of them and at the same time reserving to themselves the right to reject what they teach. This will continue as long as the Muslims do not produce their own text-books which a good Muslim teacher can assimilate himself and also elucidate.

It can be seen from this that the question of teacher-training cannot be wholly divorced from the question of curricula and text-books. They are bound up with each other, but pending the production of the right kind of text-books, a trained teacher can do a great deal with the material available to him to impart to his charges the desired kind of education. For let us not forget that whatever materials the teacher handles, it is the way he interprets them and uses them which counts for more than what they seem to offer. A good teacher can convert even inadequate materials to his own purposes provided he himself has had the right kind of training and can bring to bear upon his interpretation of the books from which he teaches the right kind of outlook.

This means that teachers should be trained according to a new methodology. The methodology of the West, in which the religious or moral approach is decried in teaching both arts and science subjects should be discarded and a new method should be evolved which takes into consideration religious and moral questions. This is not an easy task. As education is mainly morally and spiritually purposeful and not merely materially functional, the moral and spiritual impact of both the content of what is taught and the method of teaching it should be taken into consideration in teaching all subjects. Just as the content has to be assessed and graded, methods have to be formulated and applied. After all, education has become the chief means of moulding the attitudes of younger generations and initiating social change through them.

To sum up, we would once again emphasize that the teacher must be above all a committed person imbued with the right kind of moral outlook, possessed of a warm personality and capable of inspiring an enthusiasm among his learners for what he teaches and practises. This is the Islamic ideal which needs to be revived in full if the drift towards moral anarchy is to be arrested.

Extracts

1. Defining the Principles, Purposes and Policies for Teacher Education

Dr. N. A. Baloch: from *Reconstruction of Teacher Education in Islamic Society*

Dr. N. A. Baloch is Secretary for Culture in the Government of Pakistan and has had first-hand experience of teaching as a University professor and organizing teacher education as Vice-Chancellor of Sind University, Hyderabad, Pakistan. He gives in his essay a detailed analysis of the responsibilities of Muslim teachers and shows how they differ from those of their non-Muslim counterparts. We have selected from this essay only the basic principles to draw the attention of readers to the conviction of the editors of this series, first that 'education' is far more complex and comprehensive than 'instruction' or 'training' and second, that as Islam demands an integral relationship between faith and action (*iman* and *'amal*) teacher education should produce committed teachers aware of their accountability to God and society.

The objectives of teacher education in a Muslim Society will have a basic unity in fundamentals and variations in application. In order to determine the role of the teacher and the nature and objectives of teacher education, each society (country) will have

   (i) to arrive at its own consensus regarding the Guiding Principles for the Educational System to be derived from the Foundational Sources;

  (ii) to assess its own needs and problems under the conditions; and

 (iii) to determine its own 'strategy' of application in terms of specific objectives, policies and procedures to be followed in the light of the 'Guiding Principles'.

In view of their implications, the two 'Guiding Principles' may be resolved into specific 'achievement goals', as follows.

The first principle implies:

1. Commencing the educative process with faith in One Supreme Creator of all and confirming and consolidating the faith continuously to the very end.

2. Acquisition of more and more 'new' knowledge in terms of information, facts, skills, understandings and insights.
3. Ability to study Man and all that concerns him.
4. Ability to study the Universe and all its aspects.
5. Ability to think and continue the process of search and research leading to the discovery of the ultimate truth and reality of the Laws of God which operate in the world of Man and in the rest of the Universe.

The second principle implies:

6. Ability to integrate knowledge and its application.
7. Ability to improve oneself to become a useful member of the family, community and society.
8. Ability to engage in productive work for lawful earning in order to be able to contribute to the well-being of the family, community and country.
9. Ability to study and identify the needs and problems of society.
10. Ability to participate in a practical programme of action to contribute one's best to the improvement of society.
11. Ability to develop specific skills and understandings to be able to contribute specifically to the most pressing problems of society, such as educational advancement, economic development, health improvement, and cooperative community action to be able to govern the country and safeguard independence.
12. Ability to develop and use the resources, both human and material, for the continuous improvement of the society.

As a general guideline, *the preparation of teachers is to be directly related to the educational objectives to be achieved in the light of the basic 'Guiding Principles' and the 'specific achievement goals' set for the different levels of education.*

With these preliminaries stated, it is proposed to suggest a set of criteria for the recruitment, education, employment of teachers and the assessment of teachers work in a Muslim Society. It may, however, be made clear that neither is this list an exhaustive one, nor is the formulation of each 'Criterion' a final one. These Criteria are being proposed to stimulate thinking and call attention to some of the basic requirements for teacher education. It is necessary that such criteria should be adopted as 'policy decisions' in order to give a focus and direction to the programme of teacher education in a Muslim Society. Also it is necessary that the 'Criteria' and the 'policy decisions' should emerge from the basic convictions and consensus of society rather than be adopted or imposed as administrative measures on the basis of expediency.

I. *A Muslim Society Ensures Full Supply of Good Teachers Within Its Educational System.*

II. *A Muslim Society believes in the worth of the Teacher and recognizes his/her Special Role and Status in the Educational System and in Society.*

III. *A Muslim Society recognizes that formulating the Curriculum, planning and conducting the teaching learning procedures, certifying the students' accomplishment, and managing and directing the educational institutions are essentially the privilege and the responsibility of the teacher.*

IV. *A Muslim Society believes that the teacher in the Islamic Education System is a 'committed teacher' and therefore, balances his special responsibility with his accountability.*

V. *A Muslim Society believes that the worth of a teacher lies both in his personal accomplishments and in his professional competence.*

VI. *A Muslim Society believes in the life-long work and competence of the teacher, maintains him accordingly and provides him with continued opportunities to advance himself in knowledge and understanding for continuous improvement of his teaching procedures and the better guidance of the young, and for self-improvement and better service to society.*

The Need for a New Type of Broad-based, Integrated Institution

Under the Islamic education system, purposeful, broad-based education takes precedence over specialization in the case of the teacher. The teacher in a Muslim society is not a narrow specialist or a technician to be trained separately in a separate institution. No separate institutions were established for the training of teachers as part of the educational system in a Muslim Society. A teacher was not being 'trained' but he was being 'educated'; he was not being 'isolated' but 'associated'. *Murāfiqah* or 'associated learning', particularly emphasized by the Shafa'ite School of Thought, envisaged the development of social intelligence in the student so that he could become an efficient member of the Islamic community. It could be inferred that the theory and practice of education in early Muslim society was orientated more towards the development of the teacher into what may be described in modern terminology as a 'social scientist' in so far as his professional work was concerned. All students grew up as 'learners' and 'teachers' in their own spheres of work and, as such, all were educated together.

This was a distinctive contribution of Muslim educational thought and practice, the importance of which has come to be recognized in some new trends in those modern educational systems in which the training of teachers was for long advocated as a 'specialization' to be accomplished in 'separate' institutions. The narrow concept of 'training' teachers in separate institutions, and in isolation, is now giving way to the formation of integrated and broad-based institutions, and the new trend in the U.S.A. is already contributing to the 'demise of separation in teacher education'. In the U.S.S.R., there are special Pedagogical Institutes, but these are highly developed, university level institutions.

2. The Muslim Teacher in a Secular Environment

Dr. Abdul Halim Khaldoon Kinany: from *Producing Teachers for Islamic Education*

Dr. Abdul Halim Khaldoon Kinany who was born in Syria has lived in Paris since his retirement from UNESCO as Director of Higher Education. He would like Muslim teachers to be so trained as to be able to act as a counterweight to the false attractions of Western culture.

One of the main objectives of most teachers' colleges is to produce teachers for secular schools which have separated religious teaching from general education and allotted a small number of periods for its teaching each week. Thus it is taught like an historical subject or a subject among many subjects, not as a subject superior to all others and upon which all subjects should depend for their spiritual nourishment. By virtue of this they acquire a great influence on the lives of individuals and groups, elevate them to high levels of virtue and good behaviour, and ensure their performance in harmony with natural laws and the secrets of the universe.

The contemporary teacher does not possess the status and influence which his predecessors used to possess. This is partly because many specialists make the same claim, as he does, to knowing the nature of students and how to direct them, such as physicians, psychologists, sociologists, and mass leaders. Another reason is that he is a civil servant whose freedom is limited and who is not given the opportunity to introduce new methods of teaching and to discover fresh ideas about instructing students. Also, his salary is low, his income is limited, and his social contacts are few because he is imprisoned in his school.

Those who discuss the innovation of pedagogy and the development of teachers' colleges can be divided into three groups.

The first group is satisfied with imitating the old. Although this group forms its principles on a sound basis, it has to benefit from the modern world which stands for organized thought and a scientific and technological approach to problems.

Another group regards with admiration the gigantic rise of the West, its wealth and power, so it prefers to adopt its principles, to imitate the West closely, and to establish its educational schools on models provided by the West. This group is small in Muslim countries, and will remain small, because the Islamic *Ummah* is genuine and had deep roots; it will not discard its personality and adopt another instead.

The third group is the largest in number, and it is waiting to welcome educationists who are capable of bringing about an awakening in Muslim society by coordinating Islamic and Western education, and by training teachers in a way that they together with their students can benefit from the inspiration of religion as well as from the guidance of science; from the rules of moral conduct as well as from the power of technology; from the specialization of the scientist and the comprehensive and broad outlook of the religious.

Chapter Seven

The Language Problem

Arabic, the Lingua Franca of the Muslim World

The language problem in Muslim education is a consequence of the pivotal position that Arabic occupies in Islam. The question that educationists face is whether a good Islamic education is at all possible without a knowledge of Arabic. This presents no difficulty in countries whose native language is Arabic but the greater part of the Muslim world today consists of populations which speak a diversity of languages other than Arabic. We have millions of Muslims in the South Asian sub-continent speaking principally Urdu and Bengali; we have the huge area stretching from Malaysia to Indonesia where the principal language is Malaysian or Indonesian. Then we have the countries to the south of Sudan where there exist a multiplicity of languages; among them the best known in the outside world are Swahili and Hausa. This by no means exhausts the list of languages in the Islamic world. The two others which we have not so far mentioned and which constitute a very important part of the Islamic heritage are Persian and Turkish.

Down the centuries, whatever the local language, the principal emphasis in Islamic education has been on the learning of Arabic. This worked as long as the numbers to be dealt with were comparatively small. Now that we have to deal with thousands of pupils who are not expected to develop into specialists or scholars and who, after a few years of schooling, will enter various professions and occupations, the problem is what can we expect these learners to do. Can it be expected that they devote enough time to the learning of Arabic, which in many cases belongs to an entirely different linguistic family from the language locally spoken? How much Arabic can they possibly learn in the time at their disposal if at the same time they are to acquire a minimum literacy in order to be able to live usefully?[1]

Considering the paramount importance of Arabic in the Islamic scheme, it is convenient to classify all learners into two groups. The first group consists of those who can be expected to develop into scholars and who can acquire a reasonable mastery of Arabic so as to have the ability to read and understand the Quran and the teachings of the Prophet. The other group includes those who require to have an acquaintance with Arabic for the sake of the moral effect which it will have on their characters. A Muslim should be able to read the Quran even without being able to understand the words, because the ability to read the Quran itself has been known to evoke in people a response to the teachings of Islam which sociologically has been very valuable. Beyond this most of these people will hardly go but provided they learn in their childhood to respond to the music of the Arabic consonants and vowels, and to the rhythms of the Quran, they will continue throughout their lives to have an emotional attachment to it.

The class which we have described as one of specialist scholars again falls into two divisions. There will certainly be among them people who will want to study subjects other than languages and might feel that the time devoted to the study of a classical language will not be of much help. So here again two standards are necessary; those who study the sciences could be permitted a lower degree of proficiency than those who are following the Arts. It must be emphasized that it is not exactly the academic relevance of Arabic to the subjects they study in school or college which is of material importance in this context. What is important is that to have the moral training which in our judgement young Muslims should have, they must acquire some grounding in Arabic in order not to be cut off from the sources of their culture and morality.

One of the recent phenomena in Muslim countries outside the Arabic speaking world is the alienation of large groups of Muslims from their heritage, not because of any lack of faith but entirely due to a neglect of Arabic. The result often is that when in adult life a person so alienated awakens to the importance of Arabic as a source of culture, he finds it impossible to bridge the gap created by the period of neglect in his early life. How far this has gone on is shown by the fact that today in many parts of the non-Arabic speaking world dedicated Muslims depend for their knowledge of the teachings of the Quran and the Prophet upon translations in European languages. There must be hundreds among the educated population of Pakistan, India and Bangladesh – and this must also be true of Malaysia and Indonesia – whose knowledge of Islam is entirely limited to the translations they have studied. This is not a healthy state of affairs. If we believe in the importance of the continuity of our cultural heritage we must see to it that every educated Muslim youth belonging to the second group acquires more than a nodding acquaintance with the Arabic language. But this does not dispense with the necessity for translations. Realistically speaking, no matter what we do, it cannot be expected that every person who learns Arabic will also learn it adequately so as to be able to read fluently not only the Quran and the Hadith but also the commentaries. They would consequently need translations to strengthen their understanding.

Translation

The moment the question of translation is broached we are confronted with a problem which is probably peculiar to Islam. Every Muslim agrees that the Quran itself as the word of God is untranslatable, not only in the ordinary sense in which all great literary works are untranslatable, but because its meaning cannot be divorced from its rhythms and the incomparable harmony which its sounds create. So while for an understanding of the lexical meaning of the words used in the Quran a person may depend upon translations, he must never forget that the translation he studies is not and cannot be a substitute for the original which is more than a mere assemblage of words and verses.

Every possible effort must therefore be made to insist that while on the one hand a knowledge of Arabic graded to suit the abilities of the two classes of learners we have mentioned, must form an essential part of any curriculum intended for Muslim schools and universities, we also need a broad-based programme of translations which will aim at two objects: (1) to make available to those who do not speak Arabic the immense wealth of literature in this language produced over the last fifteen hundred years; and (2) to translate into Arabic works in the principal languages of the Islamic world which have made a tremendous contribution to the elucidation of Islam. Turkish, Persian, Urdu, Bengali and Malaysian are all rich in Islamic literature but most of it is unknown to the Arabic speaking world with the result that when a Muslim in the Arab world tries to assess Islamic contributions to culture he may quite unwittingly overlook what has been done outside the orbit of Arabic.[2]

Other Languages of the Muslim World and the Language Policy

In recent times works on Islam in ever increasing numbers have begun to appear even in European languages such as English, French, German, Italian and Spanish. Some of these works are by scholars known as orientalists and some are by European Muslims. In either case they need to be read and understood. Some of them are works by people whose obvious purpose is to malign Muslims or denigrate Islam, but even where this happens it is necessary for Muslims to know and understand what is being said about them by those who do not profess Islam and what can be done to answer such criticisms. Looked at in this perspective, the language policy to be followed in Islamic education acquires a degree of importance which one would not normally suspect. It is a policy which must be formulated with great care. As the size of the Islamic world widens and new peoples with new languages enter the fold of Islam the language problem will grow more and more complex, but as long as we do not lose sight of the central importance of Arabic it should not be impossible to arrive at a clear-cut policy. This should be a policy in which, with Arabic at the centre, there could be other languages grouped around it in order of their importance and given their due credit in any scheme of Islamic education.

A further question which in this connection needs to be discussed in the early stages is the relation that Arabic should bear to the mother tongue of the non-Arabic speaking people. As is well known, one of the features of traditional Islamic education was an insistence on the learning of Arabic which sometimes meant only learning the alphabet and acquiring the ability to chant a few verses from the Quran – even before a child was taught his own language. We are speaking of course of the non-Arabic speaking areas. As long as these areas had to tackle only two languages, that is Arabic and the mother tongue, few complications arose but, with the advancement of science and technology and having regard to the fact that these advances come principally from the non-Muslim West, most Muslim countries have been compelled to insist that students learn a European language. This immediately adds a third language to the programme. Then there are countries like Pakistan which have local languages and a national language. In such cases the picture becomes even more complex. The child has to learn his local language, his national language, a European language and also Arabic. How far is it practicable to have a four language programme? How are pupils going to respond to it and what exactly would be the quality of education if a high level of instruction and proficiency is enforced in the case of all four languages? A solution must be sought in the light of the future careers of pupils. Those who are destined to leave school after the primary stage, and they will continue to be a majority, will not most probably learn a European language. So in this event the number of languages to be learnt will at the most be three: the local language, Arabic and a smattering of the national language. It is usually only those who have a higher education who will find it necessary to learn all four. Again the degree of proficiency they attain will vary according to the subjects they study. Those who specialize in the study of Islam will naturally need a much better knowledge of Arabic than the average graduate.

The language problem in education consequently resolves itself into that of deciding what the priorities should be for a Muslim youth. He has to have Arabic. He cannot do without his mother tongue, he will need to learn his national language if the national language is other than his mother tongue, and in addition to all this he will need a European language.

In the Arabic speaking world the problem is much simpler. The Arabic speaking young man will need to know only his mother tongue and a European language, but scholars even in the Arabic speaking world should cultivate some of the important languages of Muslim countries for a better understanding of the problems of the Muslim world as a whole. The lack of communication between the various parts of the Muslim world at the intellectual level is a serious obstacle to the unity of the Ummah. As we have seen before, Muslim intellectuals in different countries have to communicate with each other by way of European translations instead of having direct communication with one another. The man in Karachi cannot have any direct communication with his counterpart in Cairo, Tehran or Istanbul except through a European language. This state of affairs needs to be ended as soon as possible, but it can happen only when Arabic is cultivated as the principal lingua franca throughout the Islamic world and when both Arabs and non-Arabs learn each other's languages. No language can challenge the primacy of Arabic in Muslim culture but to refuse on that ground to encourage the study of foreign languages in Arab countries would be a very short-sighted policy. So while the primacy of Arabic, what we have called its central importance, is acknowledged, the Muslim world as it is constituted today must decide in favour of a more flexible approach in its assessment of linguistic problems. We have twin objects in view:

1. A strengthening of our direct knowledge of the teachings of the Quran; and
2. Consolidation of the unity of the *Ummah*.

Both call for a carefully formulated language policy free from any nationalistic bias or prejudice.

Extracts

1. The Teaching of Quranic Arabic: Means of Comprehending the Quran, the Pivot of Islamic Education and the Source of the Cultural Unity of the Muslims

His Royal Highness Prince Muhammad al-Faisal: from *The Glorious Quran is the foundation of Islamic education*

H. R. H. Prince Muhammad al-Faisal, a member of the Royal Family in Saudi Arabia, was educated at Minto University, California. He explains why the defence and preservation of Arabic must always remain the cornerstone of any system of Islamic education.

Islamic education has its own peculiar character, which distinguishes it very clearly from all other types of educational theory or practice. This distinguishing feature is due to the ambient presence and influence of the Quran on Islamic education. The Quran is, by the consensus of Muslim opinion, in the past, the present and the future, the immutable source of the fundamental tenets of Islam, of its principles, ethics and culture. It is also the perennial foundation for Islamic systems of legislation and of social and economic organization. It is last but not least the basis of both moral and general education.

This Quranic way has the distinction of connecting all disciplines of the mind with the higher principles of Islamic creed, morals, social and economic policy as well as with legal practice. The system of Islamic education is based upon the notion that every discipline and branch of knowledge, which is of benefit to society and necessary for it, should be given due attention by the Muslim community or Ummah as a whole in order to educate all or some of its members in those disciplines. Policy, of course, depends on the variable needs of society in different times and places.

From the dawn of Islam until today, many successive generations have been nurtured and taught under the aegis of the Quran. From his tender years the Muslim child begins his education by knowing how to read, then understand and commit to memory the holy text. All other facets of the curricula of Islamic education were based upon the acknowledgement of the Quran as the core, pivot and gateway of learning. It was also recognized as the spine of all discipline. This Quranic way of education has *indeed* maintained intact the particularly Islamic personality of the Ummah and preserved its basic unity of thought and culture. As long as the Quran remains the undisputed and immutable pivot of education there is an assured guarantee that the Muslim *Ummah* will keep its integrity and authentic character.

This comprehension of the Quran cannot be open to people without their being fully conversant with the language in which it was revealed. Because of this link between the Quran and the language, the Arabic that educated Arabs use preserves the tradition and purity of Classical Arabic. Without knowing this preserved Arabic idiom it is well nigh impossible to comprehend the Quran of which every expression is originally linked to what we call classical Arabic. This is a language which is open to only a few to write and speak with happiness.

The Quran is there to be understood, taught and consulted for guidance to action. But it is impossible to reach the desired understanding of the Quran without prior study of the language in which it was revealed. To maintain the language of the Quran means spreading knowledge of it, and defending it by bringing it back to its former ascendancy as a universal language; for it is the first tongue of Islam and the reservoir of all the thought, erudition and literature which are the cultural heritage of Islam. To preserve the Arabic language in its authentic form is an absolute necessity if we mean to keep the Quran whole, uncontaminated and within admissible interpretations; or in other words, fully alive and pregnant with its great legal and moral content.

When Aisha Bint Abubakar spoke of the moral character and deportment of the greatest of Messengers, she presented it in a nutshell by saying that his moral being had been the Quran, i.e., perfect and exemplary adherence to the precepts of the Quran. We shall maintain the Arabic language, not because it is the national tongue of the Arabs, but because it is the language of the Quran, and therefore the language of Islam.

2. Organic Relationship Between the Arabic Language, Muslims in Arabic and non-Arabic Speaking Countries, and Islam

Dr. S. M. Yusuf: from *The teaching of Arabic in the non-Arabic speaking Muslim world; present conditions and possibilities with reference to the ideal*

Dr. S. M. Yusuf, who was the Professor of Arabic in the University of Karachi, Pakistan, is strongly of the view that only by restoring the primacy of Arabic in Islamic education can Muslims regain their intellectual freedom.

A study of history would prove that but for Islam the Arabic language would never have spread in various parts of the world, would never have stayed and flourished as a living language, but would have declined and become as dead as Sanskrit, Greek or Latin. It may be trite to say that it was only Islam which united the Arabs and enabled them to establish a great power which had influence inside and outside the Arabian Peninsula. Even if they had been only zealous nationalists or fanatic racists, and had been driven by their pre-Islamic chauvinism to conquer their neighbours, the Persians, the Romans, the Copts, the Berbers, the Negros, and the Goths, they would not have been able to force all those foreign nations to give up their languages and use Arabic in their homes, markets, temples, schools and offices, or more than that, become Arabicized in their thinking, interests, emotions, literature, arts and customs.

One can mention the attempts of the colonialists and imperialists which we have seen and suffered from in modern times to prove the above point. The Western powers invaded many parts of the world and conquered by force of modern arms many nations of various races and religions, but they failed in their blatant and insolent attempts to exterminate the native languages of the conquered and replace them in public life by the languages of the ruling conquerors. All they could achieve was the creation by promises and threats of a particular class of stooges and hirelings. The class of people blindly adopted a foreign culture which is alien to the elements of their original personality and culture, and consequently lived in emotional isolation, and arrogantly cut themselves off from their natural roots in the national, religious and moral environment. Although that particular class still constitutes a very small proportion of the total population in every country concerned, its elite avail themselves of the foreign language for special purposes and special occasions.

Thus a student of history should not be surprised to see how Arabic spread from Iraq to Andalus after the emergence of Islam. He could easily conclude that it was Islam that attracted the people so strongly to the Quran and the language of the Quran that they voluntarily became Arabicized. The fact that non-Arabs contributed a great deal to the field of Arabic teaching, through their study of linguistic sciences, is further evidence. I should like to stress once more that we are indebted to the Quran alone for the survival of classical Arabic and the continual use of its flawless form in spoken and written communication until the present time. Thanks to God's promise 'We have without doubt, sent down the Message, and We will assuredly guard it from corruption', Arabic has not declined, perished, or faded away into colloquial dialects.

Arab-Muslim and Non-Arab-Muslim Societies: The Differences and the Common Factor between them

There are two categories of Muslim nations. The first category comprises the nations which have completely given up their original native languages in favour of Arabic for the purposes of everyday life. The second category comprises the nations which have given special attention to studying Arabic because it is the language of the Quran and Islam, and have also established it as the language of their literature and science and the medium of education in schools. Arabic has therefore become the main element in the culture of the second category, and although it is not used for the purposes of everyday life in the homes and shops, it has pushed the native languages into these corners and completely taken over the field of science, literature and education. When as years went by local languages developed and started to creep into the courts and government offices, or apologetically sneak into poetry and other literary genres, they never hoped to acquire the status of independent languages, but always attached themselves to Arabic and orbited round it. The public revered Arabic more than any language, and the elite found it indispensable for religion, general culture, science and literature.

The difference between Arab and non-Arab Muslim societies, therefore, lies in the use of Arabic. While it is used in the first category as the language of speech for the purposes of everday life, it is not used for the same purposes in the second. However, the common factor between both categories is the fact that their societies are based on Islamic law (Shari'ah). This factor logically and practically requires the establishment of a unified system of education based on Islamic studies and the Islamic language (not only the 'first' or the 'original' but the 'only'

122

Islamic language), and that is Arabic, the language of the Quran and the Prophet's Tradition.

The appropriate use of Arabic in Islamic culture and education is mainly hindered by a class of people who received modern foreign education and were trained by the colonizers to succeed them in government and administration. That class has seized the opportunity after the independence of the non-Arab Muslim countries, and has exploited its authority and influence in talking about Islam. The talk of these people is full of inaccuracies, fabrications and stray quotations. They are not even ashamed of talking about Islam although they do not know a letter of Arabic. Some of them are lawyers who have studied Roman, English, French and Swiss laws, but have never studied Arabic, the Quran, or the Prophet's Traditions, and yet they talk about Islamic law in local and international meetings. Others are historians who have studied the history of the whole world but have never studied Islamic history, and yet they talk about the history of Islam and quote secondary sources which do not help them in pronouncing the Arabic names correctly.

Such people as those who have received foreign education in non-Arab Muslim countries are the ones who refer to the English translations of the Quran, look for English translations of the Prophet's traditions, and pick up information about Islam and Islamic law from English, French and other foreign language publications which are mostly produced by Western Orientalists whose animosity towards Islam has been proved beyond any doubt. Such people as these are the ones who claim there is no need for Arabic, despise others who study Islam from its original Arabic sources, and try hard to divorce Arabic from the programmes of Islamic studies – if these programmes have to be included in curricula of colleges and universities. This attitude is a blatant violation of the sanctity of religion and an aggression against scholarly values. The situation has even reached the stage, particularly in Pakistan and India, where those who do not know Arabic at all think there is no harm in translating the Quran and its exegesis. Br. Bint Al-Shati protested very strongly against this trend when she noticed it during her visit to India. She wrote to the *Al-Ahram* newspaper calling upon governments and scholars to exert all the influence they could to protect the Holy Quran 'from the abuse of translators, the mistakes of interpreters, and the aggression of adapters'.

3. Language Policy for Muslim countries; need for the Teaching of all the Important Languages of the Muslim World

Dr. M. M. Ghaly: from *The teaching of languages in Muslim Universities*

Dr. M. M. Ghaly, Chairman of the Department of English in King Abdulaziz University at Jeddah, Saudi Arabia, discusses the importance of English in the context of Islamic education and sketches the outlines of a language policy for Muslim countries in the following extract.

The task of learning and teaching Arabic as well as other languages of the Muslim world would open before us new horizons of thought and endeavour. The word 'progress' has cast a spell over centuries of admirers both in the West as well as in Muslim lands. But a definition of the word seems to be in order here. Literally, the word means 'going forward', and if we mean by human progress this literal connotation, this is again literally true since the unfolding of human history is a progress towards an inevitable end. Progress in this sense also involves change in time and place; for as we move along, we move in both these dimensions. Old people die and new infants are born, and in this progressive change lies the secret of human existence on this earth. But when we say that 'we need reconciliation between Orthodoxy and Progress', the word 'progress' defies definition in the literal meaning as well as in the Quranic sense. If by Orthodoxy we mean the Orthodox Caliphs, then Orthodoxy should not be brought in as the negation of progress.

English is a world language. This is a fact of the modern world, mainly because it represents the power and influence of the English-speaking people in the fields of science, politics, economics, and cultural and military achievements. To stop teaching English is to sever the ties between ourselves and the modern civilized world. But we should also desist from indulging in the self-deceptive notion of preaching the gospel of trying to reach a stage where our boys and girls hope to work, think, and feel with English hands, hearts and minds.

Ever since 1936 (1355) the proposal for conducting all instruction in Higher Education in the Arab world in the language of the Quran has been on the agenda of policy makers waiting for implementation. It is high time that it was implemented, and excuses for dodging the issue are again signs of our deep-rooted hypocritical yearning for the line of least resistance. After all, bilingualism should never be achieved at the expense of our cultural survival.

A rough outline of a co-ordinated programme for the teaching of languages (in the Arab world) under such a project would run as follows:

(1) *Intermediate (Preparatory) Schools*

No other language should be taught besides Arabic up to the end of the Intermediate or Preparatory stages. The time now allotted to other languages should be given to the study of these major cultural and linguistic areas:

A. Arabic and Muslim culture.
B. History and Culture of other peoples in Asia, Africa, Europe and the Americas.

(2) *Secondary Schools*

Other language teaching should be started from the first year Secondary, and the other languages to be taught can be divided into these language groups:

A. *European languages*: English, French, Spanish and German.
B. *Islamic languages*: Turkish, Persian, Urdu and Indonesian.
C. *African and Eastern Languages*: Bantu, Swahili, Hausa and other languages of interest.

A student would choose any two of these languages, beside Arabic, his language. The first two years of study in the secondary schools should include nine hours weekly (six and three) for each of these two languages. In the third year the number of hours should be raised to 12 : 8 and 4. In the latter case it would serve the purpose best if an arrangement could be devised for establishing (in the General Certificate of Secondary Education) a new branch for languages, besides the two already existing branches of Literary and Scientific.

(3) *Higher Education*

A. A greater variety of languages should be offered at this stage; it would be contrary to the spirit of our age, contrary to our cultural commitments, and even contrary to our linguistic commitment to the language of the Quran, to have a Department of English in almost all our institutions of Higher Education.

At least three Departments of languages should be opened in all fully-fledged Universities here and elsewhere:

1. A Department of European Languages

2. A Department of Islamic Languages
3. A Department of African and Eastern Languages

4. Means of Cooperation in the Multi-Lingual Muslim World: Text-Books and Translation

(i) *Common text-books: best means of achieving a common goal and of promoting a common cultural heritage*
Dr. Syed Sajjad Husain: from *Cooperation and understanding Muslim Scholars*

Dr. S. Sajjad Husain, former Vice-Chancellor of Dacca University in East Pakistan (now Bangladesh) and currently Professor of English in King Abdulaziz University at Mecca, Saudi Arabia, advocates the preparation and use of the new set of text-books free from anti-Islamic prejudices.

Our aim being the prevention of the erosion of faith among Muslims through education, the services of the Institute of languages and the proposed libraries must be geared to the preparation of text-books which Muslim youth can study without risk of loss of faith. This will be no easy job; nor will it be practicable to replace all existing text-books by the works of Muslim scholars. It will perhaps not be necessary, either, to find replacements for all books. At the higher stages, where students have to study and consult books mainly by non-Muslim scholars, what they need is a critical awareness to alert them to the danger of unconsciously assimilating anti-Islamic values from apparently innocuous texts. This they must acquire from the training they receive in school. It is here that we cannot afford to let them depend wholly on non-Muslim writers. It should be our endeavour to provide for schools, by which we imply all pre-University institutions, an extensive set of text-books so designed and written as to give them the most up-to-date information on the subjects children study and at the same time inculcate in these children a reverence for the eternal Islamic verities.

The writing of such text-books demands intensive study and careful research by a world-wide team of Muslim scholars, who must decide what to offer to the young and how to purge their minds of erroneous notions about Islam and its history which they will be in danger of imbibing from their environment, particularly if they belong to countries which do not subscribe to Islam. Two centuries of intellectual domination by the West coupled with the general backwardness of Muslims have disposed many Muslims to view the world through non-Muslim eyes, and the result in such subjects as history, political science, philosophy and sociology has been the uncritical acceptance of attitudes which militate against the fundamentals of Islam. To counteract this, we need a team of scholars who must survey each area of knowledge carefully, spot the anti-Islamic prejudices, and recast reading material for juveniles so as to guard them from exposure to misrepresentations of fact.

It is not to be supposed that we recommend an anti-Western bias in our text-books to oppose the current anti-Islamic bias in those of the West. Far from it. We should like the young to learn the truth. But every community must take care to transmit its intellectual heritage to its young, and that precisely is the task facing Muslims. When one considers the enormous range of books in non-Muslim societies produced for the young in which attention is directed exclusively to the transmission and preservation of their past heritage, whether that heritage concerns the achievements of the Greeks, the Romans, Mediaeval Europe or ancient India, and reflect on the comparative complacency of Muslim scholars, then one receives a shock. If we are up against the danger of a general decay of faith in Islam among the younger generation, we have our own lethargy to blame for it.

It may well be asked how a central committee or board located in any one country can produce text-books for adoption in widely different regions with dissimilar linguistic backgrounds. Text-books for use by the young must necessarily be in the languages which they speak and understand. It will obviously not do to insist that whatever a child's mother tongue, he must be made to study a standard text-book written in a foreign language. What we recommend and envisage is the preparation of model texts which local scholars can either translate, where much translation is practicable, or on which they can base their own books, with such local variations as circumstances could demand. The aim is not so much the imposition of a uniform set of text-books upon entire communities of Muslim children, as the eradication of those errors and prejudices in which their present reading material abounds. This is not a task beyond the powers of a competent team of Muslim scholars working together.

(ii) *Problems of translation in a multi-lingual Muslim world and the urgent need for solving them in order to achieve mutual communication, understanding and cooperation among Muslims at all levels, scholarly, political and economic*

127

Mr. Peter Hobson: from *Translation: problems and methods*

Light on another aspect of the language problem, namely, the problem of translation, is thrown by Mr. Peter Hobson, a European Muslim. Himself an experienced linguist, who knows several European and Asian languages including Malay and Chinese, Mr. Hobson is well known for his English translations of the works of Schuon, the noted authority on comparative religion, and Titus Burckhardt, author of *The Art of Islam*.

If it is decided to produce a translation which will stand in its own right, being intended not simply for students of the original language but for a more general public – perhaps including non-Muslims whom one wishes to draw to Islam – then the following factors are, I think, relevant:

(a) The translator should be a master of his native tongue, well-versed in its various literary modes, grammatical subtleties and expressive possibilities and aware of its strengths and weaknesses, and he should then translate only into his native tongue; no depth of knowledge of the original language will compensate for lack of feeling and sensibility as regards the language into which one is translating, whereas a comparative lack of real depth in the language from which he is translating can be compensated for by good dictionaries and the advice of experts.

(b) If, for practical reasons, a translator be required to work into a tongue that is not native to him, even if this is a tongue in which he has received a large part of his education, then he must be prepared to submit his work for criticism and correction to an informed and sensitive native speaker of the tongue into which he is translating. (There are, I know, certain outstanding exceptions in the past to this rule that a man should write in, or translate into, his native language alone – and in our own day too – but they remain exceptions, and the best of them have not hesitated to submit themselves to this discipline.)

(c) In any case, and whatever his qualifications in the languages he is translating from and into, a translator should ideally be a man of virtue and some humility, for he is required to retain his linguistic and literary sensibility on the one hand and, on the other, to sacrifice his own ego to the point of faithfully transmitting ideas from one medium to another without imposing his own notions or mental colouring; and this is not always easy. Reshaping according to the exigencies of different languages is one thing, and distortion is another. It is for this reason that a translation is always best checked by a second person having appropriate qualifications in both subject and languages, and also because men are fallible and can omit or mistranslate passages from sheer tiredness, for serious translation is demanding work.

(d) A translator should, ideally, be well-versed in, and preferably favourably disposed towards, the subject with which he is dealing.

(e) A translator, having if possible the above qualifications, should first of all familiarize himself with the entire work which he hopes to translate; then, taking into account the style, quality and historical period of the original, he should decide on an appropriate form of language for translation and adhere to it consistently. In order to be able to do this, he should know the purpose for which the translation is intended; if specialized knowledge or terminology is involved he should read existing works on the same subject and learn from them.

(f) If he has time, he should first produce a translation that aims at the greatest possible fidelity to the original, and this is not, of course, necessarily the most literal translation for it is not fidelity to translate a beautiful original into an ugly reproduction in a second language in the pretended interests of exactitude. He should then check the whole and have it checked. He should then produce a polished, final version from his first one and do so – again if time allows – only after a lapse of time in which he has been able to free his mind from the idiom of the original, for this almost inevitably imposes itself to the detriment of the style of translation; paradoxically, this is particularly true when the two languages are closely related, for one is lulled into a false sense of security.

(g) Finally, all that has been said in the preceding sub-paragraphs could be qualified by saying that translators who are both qualified in the original tongue and have a reasonable mastery of their own language are not very numerous and that, if any large scale programme of translation is to be attempted, collaboration between pairs of persons – the one a master of the original and the other a master of his own tongue – is a viable method, provided each give the other his due.

NOTES

Chapter One

1. Arnold J. Toynbee: *Change and Habit: The Challenge of Our Time*, London, O.U.P., 1966, p. 21.
2. *Ibid.*, p. 19
3. *Ibid.*, p. 11.
4. Bertrand Russell: *Impact of Science on Society*, London, Allen & Unwin, 1952, p. 114.
5. Quran, 2:70
6. Quran, 2:285 'We do not distinguish between one prophet and another.'
7. *Ibid.*, II, V.
8. Karl Mannheim: *Diagnosis of Our Time*, Heinemann, London, 1943, pp. 12–17.
9. See *Conference Book*, London 1978, pp. 15–17 and pp. 88–90, both on the definition and aims of education as discussed and agreed at the Mecca Conference on Education in 1977.

Chapter Two

1. Each society interprets this idea of transmission in its own way. John Dewey's, Lenin's and Ibn Khaldun's interpretations are different from each other and from the interpretation of those modernists who consider values as entirely dependent on social change. For sociological interpretation of this transmission see Olive Banks: *The Sociology of Education*, London, 1976.
2. Hadith: The Prophet of Islam, peace and blessings of Allah be on him, said that every child is born a Muslim, it is his or her parents who turn him or her into a Christian or a Jew or an atheist.
3. 'Behold, thy Lord said to the angels: "I will create a vicegerent on earth" ', Quran 2·30.
4. 'God will raise in rank those of you who believe as well as those who are given knowledge': Quran 58:11 'The learned men are the heirs of the prophets', Hadith: *al-Bukhari*, ch. on 'Ilm, 11.

> 'The superior rank the learned man holds in relation to the worshipper is like the superior rank I hold in relation to the best of men', Hadith in *Mishkat-al-Masabih*, Vol. 1, 14.

5. Islam does not believe in racial superiority. God says: 'O mankind, we have created you male and female, and have made you races and tribes, that you may know one another' (al-Quran, 49:13).
6. That is why man is asked by God to say 'Truly, my prayer and my service of sacrifice, my life and my death are all for God, the cherisher of the Worlds' (al-Quran, 6:162). For further details about this concept see *Conference Book*, pp. 76–78.
7. For an analysis of all benefits derived from modern sciences see Bertrand Russell: *The impact of Science on Society*.

8. A large number of Western thinkers are aware of this situation: e.g., Karl Mannheim: *Diagnosis of Our Time*, London, 1943, Arnold J. Toynbee: *Civilization on Trial*, Oswald Spengler: *Decline of the West* (trans.) London, 1926 and even Bertrand Russell, a great supporter of modern science in the chapter on 'Science and Values' in *Impact of Science on Society*, *op. cit.*

9. See Frithjof Schuon: *Spiritual Perspectives and Human Facts* (trans. by Matheson), London, 1954. Seyyed Hossein Nasr: *The Encounter of Man and Nature: The Spiritual Crisis of Modern Man*, Longmans, London, 1975.

10. As presented in the *Memorandum* for the First World Conference on Muslim Education at Mecca. See *Conference Book*, *op. cit.* pp. 9–29.

11. The best example is Prophet Muhammad, peace and blessings of Allah be on him.

Chapter Three

1. Abd el-Latif Tibawi: *Islamic Education*, London, 1972 gives a brief account of its traditions and modernization in the Arab national systems. His study is confined to the Arab world.

2. This came out clearly in the surveys of modern and traditional Islamic systems of education carried out for the First World Conference on Muslim Education held at Mecca in 1977 under the supervision of Dr. Syed Ali Ashraf.

3. The present struggle in Turkey and the bloodshed in 1971 and 1972 in Bangladesh and in Indonesia have been studied by various authors. The origin of all these troubles must be seen in the attempt to secularize a religious society.

4. The destruction of Baghdad by Halaku Khan is considered by some as the beginning of this trend.

5. The total Muslim population in 1901 was more than 100 million.

6. William Hunter, an Indian Civil Servant, wrote in 1870 in *The Indian Mussulmans* (re-issued by The Comrade Publisher, 1945), p. 161 that the British policy of persecution and systematic pauperization had made a rich community poor and helpless.

7. For a detailed history of traditional Islamic education and its courses in India one has to read the official Education Commission reports.

8. See Tibawi, *op. cit.* for a detailed discussion of what happened after the modernization of national systems. Though Tibawi seems to think that 'a great deal of Islamic and Arabic spirit' is infused in each of these systems, he admits: 'Islam or Arab nationalism in education has now become a sterile question. More relevant is the practical question of whether the modern system produces better leaders' (p. 224).

Chapter Four

1. *Conference Book*, London, 1978. p. 88.

2. See Hossein Nasr: Chapter II on 'The Basis of the Teaching System and the Educational Institutions' in *Science and Civilization in Islam*, Mentor Books, New York, 1970, pp. 59–91 for further details.

3. See Al-Farabi: *Enumeration of the Sciences* known in the West as *De Scientiis* in Latin and Hebrew translations. Avicenna: *The Book of Healing* and Treatise on the *Classifications of the Intellectual Sciences* and Al-Ghazzali: *The Book of Knowledge*, trans. by Nabih Amin Faris, Ashraf, Lahore, 1962 (from the Arabic original *Ihya Ulum al-Deen*). Ibn Khaldun: *The Muqaddima: An Introduction to History*, translated from the Arabic by Franz Rosenthal, New York, 1958.

4. As explained by Hossein Nasr in *Science and Civilization in Islam*, pp. 62–64.

5. *Ibid*. p. 74.

6. *Ibid*. pp. 74–79 (quoted as an extract under Chapter Two of the present book).

7. See *The Division and Methods of Sciences* translated by A. Maurer, Toronto, 1963.

8. See F. H. Hilliard: 'The Legacy of Christianity in the Schools' in *Christianity in Education*, London, 1966, pp. 13–28 for a detailed description of this process.

9. *Ibid*. See also R. H. Tawney: *Religion and the rise of Capitalism*, Penguin 1938, p. 273.

10. See also *Conference Book* pp. 21–23 for a short note on psychology and history and pp. 88–90 for recommendations.

11. Muhammad Iqbal: *The Reconstruction of Religious Thought in Islam*, Ashraf Publications, Lahore, 1971, p. 154.

12. This doctrine resembles the well-known theories of the ancient Hindu social order and the theories of Plato and the thinkers of the Christian Middle Ages. All of them regard social institutions as 'means to the perfectibility of the individual'. That ideal is one's real self which one must constantly try to know. From the Sufistic point of view each individual manifests an *ism*, name or quality or power of God and each individual ought to realize his vocation by comprehending that *ism*. That is his *ism-i-azam*. From the social point of view, however, the similarity between Hindu and Muslim viewpoints ends there. According to the Hindu concept the caste-system 'is divinely sanctioned' (see *Bhagavad-Gita*, Chs. IV and V as summarized by Ananda Coomaraswamy in 'Religious Basis of the Forms of Indian Society' in *East and West and Other Essays*, Colombo, pp. 28–29); man has to fulfil his vocation within that order. Islam conceives an 'open society' which is given a common law for interpersonal, intergroup and interracial relationships and within the orbit of that law man has to fulfil his vocation.

13. See Seyyed Hossein Nasr: *The Encounter of Man and Nature, The Spiritual Crisis of Modern Man*, London, Allen & Unwin, 1968.

Chapter Five

1. The education conference at Mecca divided knowledge into two categories: (1) Perennial knowledge based on the Divine revelation in the Quran and Sunnah and (2) acquired knowledge including humanities, social and natural sciences. See *Conference Book*, p. 78.

2. The archetype is the essence, the idea, the ideal form that is in the object and is the source of the external form. It is that which has been manifested in creation. As the Divine Will is the creative force, as God alone brings into actuality that which we see in the sensible world, each and every created object in essence exists in the Will of God. This idea is universally accepted by traditional thinkers of the West and the East. For Hindu and Buddhist versions see Ananda K. Coomaraswamy: *Why Exhibit Works of Art, The Aims of Indian Art* and *The Transformation of Nature in Art*. For the Christian concept see also St. Thomas Aquinas, *Summa Theologica* I, ('imitating nature in her manner of operation'). For the Islamic concept see Frithjof Schuon, *The Transcendent Unity of Religions*, London 1953 ('It is solely and exclusively traditional art . . . transmitted with tradition and by tradition, which can guarantee the adequate analogical correspondence between the divine and cosmic orders on the one hand, and the human or "artistic" on the other').

3. 'It is true that if the artist has not *conformed himself* to the pattern of the thing to be made he has not really known it and cannot work originally. But if he has thus conformed himself he will be in fact expressing *himself* in bringing it forth. Not indeed expressing his "personality" as "this man" so-and-so, but himself *sub specie aeternitatis*, and apart from individual idiosyncrasy' (*Why Exhibit Works of Art*, A. K.

Coomaraswamy). Compare the same idea in St. Thomas Aquinas, *Summa Theol.* I, 91, a, 3c.

4. *Enneads*, V, 1.4.

5. Elder Olson 'An Outline of Poetic Theory', *Critics and Criticism* (abridged) R. S. Crane (ed.), Chicago 1957, p. 3.

6. John Henry Newman: *Select Discourses from The Idea of a University*, ed. by May Yardley, Cambridge University Press, 1931, 'Discourse VIII', pp. 102–120.

7. *Republic* 500E. 'The realities are seen by the eye of the Soul'. *Republic* 533D. 'The Soul alone and by itself' (*Theatatus* 186, 187). 'Gazing ever on what is authentic' (*Timaeus* 28A) . . . and 'thus by inwit (intuition) of what really is'. Quoted by Coomaraswamy in *Figures of Speech or Figures of Thought*, London, 1946, p. 38.

8. *Enneads*, IV, 4.2.

9. St. Thomas Aquinas, *Truth*, R. W. Mulligan (trans.) Chicago, 1952, q, 4, a, 4.

10. Summ. Theol. I, q, 45, a, 6.

Chapter Six

1. The supreme model is Prophet Muhammad, peace and blessings of God be on him. All teachers have to follow him and organize their lives according to his pattern.

2. That is why religious education by such people in British schools, for example, has become an information-giving process and not a character-building endeavour.

Chapter Seven

1. It requires a regular survey of languages spoken in all Muslim countries and the position of Arabic in school and university courses.

2. There is an increasing realization in the Arab world that other languages of the Muslim world should be taught in their universities. King Abdulaziz University, Jeddah, Mecca has already planned to have a section on such languages.